Without character to carry the gift, the train will run off the tracks. Without boundaries to the river, we have nothing more than runoff water. But with banks put in place, we channel the river of God's presence into purposeful use. I am one who strongly believes in the "joining of the generations" as well. There are few in the global prophetic movement who come from the rich history that R. Loren Sandford does. We have had the Elijah Task from his parents; now we have another vintage resource for this generation. *The Last Great Outpouring* is such a work.

—*James W. Goll*
Founder, God Encounters Ministries, GOLL Ideation LLC

Loren Sandford's book, *The Last Great Outpouring*, is a timely word indeed and, I might boldly add, it is a must read. There are many thought-provoking insights that will cause you to inquire of the Lord. You might discover revelations you had not previously embraced or even considered within its pages. God's love is always unshifting and unconditional, but His tone changes at times. In this season, a weightier and more serious and corrective love-filled tone will be released by the Spirit in order to bring alignment to His heart and purposes. I believe Loren Sanford has been prepared and called for such a time as this.

—*Patricia King*
Author, TV host, and minister

I have walked with R. Loren Sandford over the last ten years and recognize him as a seasoned prophetic father in the body of Christ with a proven history of integrity and prophetic accuracy. His unwavering commitment to the secret place and pure devotion to Jesus Christ makes him a reliable voice in a sea of inaccurate prophetic utterance and compromise. If you are ready for a pure prophetic vision and clarion call inviting all of us into a deeper place of hearing and obeying God, start reading *The Last Great Outpouring*. You will not be disappointed!

—*Jeremiah Johnson*
Author, TV host, and founder
Jeremiah Johnson Ministries, Maranatha School of Ministry

Loren Sandford is in touch with both the current moves of God and what we need to do to get ready for the greatest harvest of souls the world has ever known. His book is earnest and thought-provoking. We all need to prepare ourselves for the tsunami of glory coming.

—*Cindy Jacobs*
Founder, Generals International

With so many doom and gloom prophets making a name for themselves on the Internet, R. Loren Sandford's *The Last Great Outpouring* stands out as a beacon of hope for the greatest outpouring the church has ever seen. The next great move of God will be beyond anything eye has seen or ear has heard or has entered into the heart of man. Prophetically, Loren sees the coming outpouring and helps us to prepare for what must happen before we see it. He handles issues like judgment and mercy skillfully so readers can grasp the events that are about to unfold and ready our hearts to answer the call to become nation-changers. I highly recommend this book!

—*Jennifer LeClaire*
Author, *The Making of a Prophet*
Senior Leader, Awakening House of Prayer

THE
LAST GREAT
OUTPOURING

PREPARING FOR AN
UNPRECEDENTED MOVE OF GOD

R. LOREN SANDFORD

WHITAKER
HOUSE

All Scripture quotations are taken from the updated *New American Standard Bible*®, NASB®, © 1960, 1962, 1963, 1968, 1971, 1972, 1973, 1975, 1977, 1995 by The Lockman Foundation. Used by permission. (www.Lockman.org).

Boldface type in the Scripture quotations indicates the author's emphasis.

THE LAST GREAT OUTPOURING
Preparing for an Unprecedented Move of God

New Song Church and Ministries
8242 Pecos Street
Denver, CO 80221
www.newsongchurchandministries.org
www.rlorensandford.com
loren@newsongchurchandministries.org

ISBN: 978-1-64123-488-7
eBook ISBN: 978-1-64123-489-4

Printed in the United States of America
© 2020 by R. Loren Sandford

Whitaker House
1030 Hunt Valley Circle
New Kensington, PA 15068
www.whitakerhouse.com

Library of Congress Cataloging-in-Publication Data (Pending)

1 2 3 4 5 6 7 8 9 10 11   ⅏   27 26 25 24 23 22 21 20

CONTENTS

FOREWORD

I received a prophetic dream recently in which I found myself in a parking lot following a uniformed officer who was handing out parking tickets. I could not believe how many tickets this gentleman was handing out for "illegal parking." When I asked what was happening, he turned to me and said, "Most of these cars do not have authorization to park here, although they look like they do." Confused because of the amount of cars he ticketed, I said, "Well, do any of these cars have authorization to park here?" He replied, "Only those that have passed an internal certified inspection. My job depends on my ability to distinguish between the cars that look the part on the outside from those that have actually passed the state standard from the inside."

As I prayed into the dream, God said to me:

"We are entering into an era in the body of Christ where the ability to discern the difference between the true and the false will become increasingly difficult. *The next decade will be marked by HARVEST, yet My people must understand that with harvesting comes an exposing of deception (tares) and a love for the truth like never before (wheat).* At times, that which is manufactured and counterfeit will be passed off as genuine and trustworthy, just as that which is anointed and appointed by Me will seek to be passed off as null and void.

"There is a satanic assault being loosed in the body to confuse and bring great disillusionment to the saints concerning those leaders and saints in whom they can trust and those they cannot. A Bearing of False Witness against the Brethren shall rise. Remember, I hate a false witness who speaks lies and the one who sows discord among the brethren (Proverbs 6:16–19).

"You must take great pains in these days to become lovers of the truth. *Buy truth, and do not sell it* (Proverbs 23:23). Those who love the truth in the last days shall be the most hated for lies and falsehood will abound. Be very careful in your discerning that you do not become hasty in your judgments, nor should you judge by outward appearance, for the Lord looks at the heart. Even now, there are individuals who you should be in relationship with that you are not because you have been given a false witness report about them, just as there are people you are connected to that must be cut off if you are to love the truth more than personal preference. Because of this intense season of harvesting over the next decade, I'm calling My people to an ascended lifestyle. It's time to come before My throne. Only I know the motivations, intentions, and thoughts of the human heart. Without spending time in My presence, you will never be able to discern the true and the false, the wheat from the tares, says the Lord."

I have been closely following the life and ministry of R. Loren Sandford for almost the last decade. His fatherly heart and prophetic purity is one of the greatest needs that we have in the body of Christ right now. More than that, Loren has been a faithful shepherd in the house of God and his commitment to covenant family and unity permeates every chapter of this book. As I read, I was overcome with excitement as well as sobriety. Loren has articulated a very real and inspiring vision of the days ahead, yet like a true prophetic father, he has also been faithful to warn us of the potential dangers and pitfalls that can await the body of Christ if we are not discerning. I was deeply stirred by his presentation of such a weighty yet clear prophetic portrait of the coming days. This prophetic vision has the ability to bring great impact in every nation of the earth.

Indeed, the wheat and the tares are growing up together in the global church. The false and the true, the holy and the profane, are simultaneously arising. Our need to discern, use the wisdom of God, and prepare for the last great outpouring of the Holy Spirit has never been greater. Pay special attention to chapters nine and thirteen. I highly recommend R. Loren Sandford, his ministry, and the prophetic anointing upon his life. If God has saved His best for last, then I am so incredibly grateful that He has chosen and raised up a prophetic father like Loren for such a time as this. Prepare to be encouraged, challenged, and filled with hope for the days ahead. I know I was!

—*Jeremiah Johnson*
Founder, Heart of the Father Ministry
Best-selling author
www.jeremiahjohnson.tv

INTRODUCTION

After four hundred years of prophetic silence, God sent John the Baptist to announce the coming of Messiah Jesus, the baptism He would bring, and the inbreaking of the kingdom of God on the earth. In response, people streamed to the Jordan River to hear his words and be baptized by him in the Jewish ritual *mikveh* bath for cleansing from sin and defilement. John's calling was to prepare the people for the coming glory.

Our God is nothing if not consistent—the same yesterday, today, and forever. As in the days leading to the return of Jesus, He therefore continues to send messengers in advance to announce coming moves of the Spirit in order to prepare His people to receive. Although I make no claim to anything like the stature of John the Baptist or any other biblical prophet, I have written this book in that spirit. God is about to do something huge, wonderful, and even unprecedented in scope and impact. In fact, I believe it to be the last great outpouring before the Lord's return. It is my desire to help the body of Christ to prepare for the glory.

I am not alone in this. The words I've written are not exclusive to me. Increasing numbers of others, although largely in the minority in terms of what I have to say, have been releasing similar words. May God's people have ears to hear!

1

THE TEMPLE OF THE LORD: GOD'S VISION

I have long recognized that the church in the world, at least in my own nation, has lost its voice. In contrast with that awareness, I rejoice in both the scriptural promise and my own sense of anticipation that an outpouring of the Spirit of God such as the world has never seen is about to be made manifest. I see the emergence of a holy remnant, centered in the heart of the Father, ever more conformed to the image of the Son and rising in the spirit of Daniel and Joseph to high places of influence. According to Isaiah 60, as nations stream to the brightness of our rising, we will influence even rulers and kings.

Essential to this move of God is the restoration of His vision for the temple of the Lord, a vision having its roots in the Old Testament and carrying forward into the New Testament. I therefore begin with the prophet Haggai, who prophesied in the last decades of the sixth century BC in the years following

Israel's return to their land after seventy years of exile in Babylon. Upon their return, they found a land utterly destroyed and thus they began the arduous task of rebuilding.

Apparently, by the time of Haggai's ministry, some years had passed. There had been plenty of time to begin rebuilding God's house and yet the temple of the Lord, which had been the center of their lives before Babylon ravaged the land, continued to lie in ruins.

Things weren't going well for the nation. Economically, times were hard and nothing seemed to be working. Haggai therefore came on the scene with a prophetic burden to explain things on God's behalf, confront the people with their failure to prioritize the building of the temple, and get things working again by setting spiritual priorities in order.

> THE CHURCH IN OUR DAY HAS BEEN RAVAGED AND DIMINISHED
> IN INFLUENCE UNDER PRESSURE FROM
> THE IDOLATROUS CULTURE THAT SURROUNDS US.

IT'S TIME FOR US TO REBUILD

I would suggest that the church in our day has been ravaged and diminished in influence under pressure from the idolatrous culture that surrounds us. Figuratively speaking, a remnant is even now returning from exile. It's time to rebuild on a biblical foundation and construct a temple adequate to contain the outpouring God is about to send.

To Israel, Haggai said:

Thus says the LORD of hosts, "This people says, 'The time has not come, even the time for the house of the LORD to be rebuilt.'"　　　　　　　　　　　　　　　(Haggai 1:2)

The people responded with something like this: "Haggai! Don't you understand!? The economy is terrible and we're all struggling and you want us to build a temple! We'll build the temple when the time is right, but first, we have to set all our own affairs in order and get the economic pressure off of us. Then we can turn our attention to constructing a temple."

Haggai presented his prophecy as a conversation between the people and God. As the people voiced their reasons for not giving and not taking time to rebuild the temple, God answered them through Haggai. As we examine God's response, please remember that there never was and never will be so much as one thing God does or says that fails to flow from His love for us for our benefit.

Then the word of the LORD came by Haggai the prophet, saying, "Is it time for you yourselves to dwell in your paneled houses while this house lies desolate?" Now therefore, thus says the LORD of hosts, "Consider your ways! You have sown much, but harvest little; you eat, but there is not enough to be satisfied; you drink, but there is not enough to become drunk; you put on clothing, but no one is warm enough; and he who earns, earns wages to put into a purse with holes."   (Haggai 1:3–6)

In other words, God said to them, "I *do* understand. I see your struggles. Now let Me explain why you're struggling so that I can get you out of it and release a blessing."

Thus says the LORD of hosts, "Consider your ways! Go up to the mountains, bring wood and rebuild the temple, that I may be pleased with it and be glorified," says the LORD. "You look for much, but behold, it comes to little; when you bring it home, I blow it away. Why?" declares the LORD of hosts, "Because of My house which lies desolate, while

> *each of you runs to his own house. Therefore, because of you
> the sky has withheld its dew and the earth has withheld its
> produce. I called for a drought on the land, on the moun-
> tains, on the grain, on the new wine, on the oil, on what the
> ground produces, on men, on cattle, and on all the labor of
> your hands."*   (Haggai 1:7–11)

God prescribed a remedy, a course of action, and the people responded positively.

> *Then Zerubbabel the son of Shealtiel, and Joshua the son
> of Jehozadak, the high priest, with all the remnant of the
> people, obeyed the voice of the LORD their God and the
> words of Haggai the prophet, as the LORD their God had
> sent him. And the people showed reverence for the LORD.
> Then Haggai, the messenger of the LORD, spoke by the com-
> mission of the LORD to the people saying, "I am with you,"
> declares the LORD.*   (Haggai 1:12–13)

You might ask, how could a structure, a collection of sticks and stones, have meant so much to God that a curse would rest on the land until it was restored? Was the structure, the building, really the issue? The answer is no. The significance of the temple went well beyond just the structure, and involved purposes much deeper and more important than the man-made building.

God doesn't change. The God of the Old Testament is the God of the New Testament—same heart, same will, and same love. As we move into the New Testament, the outward forms of things change, but the substance remains because God's heart remains the same. If you adequately understand the temple, then you see and understand the love in God's plans for it. The lessons embedded in the word that came through Haggai stand firm and deep for all eternity.

> THE LESSONS EMBEDDED IN THE WORD THAT CAME THROUGH
> HAGGAI STAND FIRM AND DEEP FOR ALL ETERNITY.

THE TEMPLE'S HEART AND RESOURCES

The Old Testament temple was more than just a building in which to worship. It was a rallying place of identity and relationship for the people, a place where, whether you were rich or poor, highborn or lowly, you knew, *This is mine because this is ours.* More importantly, it was a resource center for the nation as a whole, a storehouse for the benefit of all the people to supply at least four kinds of resources that were essential to Israel—resources that remain essential to *us.*

SPIRITUAL RESOURCES

"For the lips of a priest should preserve knowledge, and men should seek instruction from his mouth; for he is the messenger of the Lord *of hosts"* (Malachi 2:7). Both then and now, people need instruction in who God is and how to relate to Him. From the beginning, God intended the temple to be a center from which His designated priests would communicate that revelation to the people.

> And many peoples will come and say, "Come, let us go up to the mountain of the Lord, to the house of the God of Jacob; that He may teach us concerning His ways and that we may walk in His paths." For the law will go forth from Zion and the word of the Lord from Jerusalem.   (Isaiah 2:3)

God created us for connection with Him. The priests offered sacrifices on behalf of the people to keep them connected with God in offerings of thanksgiving and to cleanse away the barriers that sin erected. God commissioned the priests to teach the people how to connect with Him, so they could learn His will and nature, walk in His paths, and live.

As the temple was a place of worship, a place to connect with God, not just in sacrifice, but in glorious song, so there will come a renewal of worship to the New Testament church in our day. A tremendous burst of creativity, such as that which produced the Psalms, is on the horizon. It will be the last days' *"new song"* (Revelation 14:3) that only the sold-out remnant can learn. At the dedication of Solomon's original temple, the power of the glory cloud rendered the priests unable to even stand. Similarly, the coming burst of worship in these last days will be accompanied by supernatural signs and wonders for the healing of those the Lord calls.

> THE COMING BURST OF WORSHIP IN THESE LAST DAYS WILL BE ACCOMPANIED BY SUPERNATURAL SIGNS AND WONDERS.

The time is coming when the growing remnant will shine so brightly with supernatural kingdom power and love that *many peoples will come* to seek out those places where the presence of God will be manifest. The temple of the Lord on the earth will be restored in a multitude of points of light strategically placed around the globe because the glory of the Lord and the truth of His love and power will go forth from a restored spiritual temple.

MATERIAL RESOURCES

The Old Testament temple stood as the center of the nation's welfare program. The hungry went there for food in times of need. The poor found sustenance and help at the house of God.

People today foolishly argue over whether or not tithing is New Testament, but there was and remains a purpose for it that transcends the question of being under the law...or under grace. Malachi 3:10 reads, *"Bring the whole tithe into the storehouse, so that there may be food in My house."*

It wasn't that God needed the people's money or their produce for Himself. He owns the cattle on a thousand hills and never needs to eat anyway. Obviously, the temple required maintenance, as does any physical structure, and the priests who served needed a means of making a living. But above all, there had to be food and resources in the Lord's house for the care of the poor and needy. This was the reason for the tithe, selflessly rendered, not for the promise of personal prosperity or to avoid the curse.

Again, the issue of God's love found expression through the temple, a center that people could identify and know they had a place to go for help. To withhold the tithe was to starve the poor, to leave the house of God without resources to care for those the Lord loves. I don't believe there's been any change in God's will on that matter because God Himself never changes. This remains God's plan in love for His church.

HEALING RESOURCES

How many of us realize that the Old Testament law contains multiple prescriptions for healing to be administered through the temple? For example, Leviticus 12 governs a woman's recovery from childbirth and the sacrifices to be offered for it. Leviticus 13–14 instruct the priests on how to deal with the issue of leprosy. Leviticus 15 addresses treatments for discharges from the body and prescribes sacrifices to be offered at the temple for healing and cleansing.

These are just a few examples. God intended the temple to be a healing center, and not just for physical conditions. The various sacrifices offered for sin were for the healing of broken and defiled hearts who came to repent and set right what had been wrong. Never were these instructions to be looked upon as mere ritual. Real transactions happened between God and people in the realm of the spirit. Sin in the world causes hearts and lives to be broken and shattered. God designed the temple sacrifices to cleanse sin, heal hearts and lives, and restore people to God in His love. Whether or not the people ever truly understood it, the temple stood as a place for repairing the damage caused by sin. God worked to restore lives through the services of the temple. People knew where to go to find healing.

> GOD DESIGNED THE TEMPLE SACRIFICES TO CLEANSE SIN, HEAL HEARTS AND LIVES, AND RESTORE PEOPLE TO GOD IN HIS LOVE.

In our day, we have seen five decades of revelation for the restoration of hearts and lives in what has erroneously been called *inner healing*. In the spirit of Romans 8 and 12, the better term is *transformation*. Untold thousands of lives have seen healing and change as a result. In addition, we have seen bursts of healing anointing for physical ailments, injuries, and dysfunctions. There will be more as God restores His temple in and among us.

Once more, I point out that God has not changed. There is a New Testament temple and it carries the same mandates from the heart of God as did the temple of old. No genuine revival can occur without these elements of God's eternal plan.

RELATIONAL RESOURCES

No living person born of woman is exempt from the need for relationship. And for relationship to be whole, to be as God intended, it must be a three-way phenomenon involving you, me, and God in oneness. Every one of us needs people committed to walk with us, to know us, to speak into our lives, and to stand with us in times of trouble or need. God designed the temple as a rallying point for that kind of covenant connection. People found one another there. It was everybody's home where friends connected and life was shared.

> ### GOD DESIGNED THE TEMPLE AS A RALLYING POINT FOR A COVENANT CONNECTION.

Hints are found in some of the psalms and other places. Psalm 55 expresses pain at the loss of a relationship that had been forged in the temple:

> *For it is not an enemy who reproaches me, then I could bear it; nor is it one who hates me who has exalted himself against me, then I could hide myself from him. But it is you, a man my equal, my companion and my familiar friend; we who had sweet fellowship together walked in the house of God in the throng.*   (Psalm 55:12–14)

In Psalm 50, God called for a gathering at which He would confront the people with their relational violations: "*Gather My godly ones to Me, those who have made a covenant with Me by sacrifice*" (Psalm 50:5). *Gather* is a fellowship word and *sacrifice* roots it in the temple, where worship and relationships were pursued.

This is even clearer in Psalm 68:

> *A father of the fatherless and a judge for the widows, is God in His holy habitation. God makes a home for the lonely; He leads out the prisoners into prosperity, only the rebellious dwell in a parched land.*   (Psalm 68:5–6)

Any Hebrew reading that psalm would have interpreted *habitation* as referring to the temple, the place where God made His name to dwell. Note the phrase, "*a home for the lonely.*"

The opposite of lonely is fellowship and friendship. In love, God intended the temple to be a rallying point for connections between people, a place where love would grow and no one would feel alone and friendless.

God has not changed His mind. A great outpouring of the Spirit is coming and at its heart will be renewed love among God's people that will resound across nations and draw a lonely and isolated generation to the Lord. In the natural world, we know where to buy groceries and fill the tanks of our cars with fuel. Shouldn't we equally know where to find fellowship, a home, oneness with others, and people to walk with, grow with, and share life with? God loves us, but that love will never be complete until it's shared. *"I was glad when they said to me, 'Let us go to the house of the* LORD*'"* (Psalm 122:1).

THE NEW TESTAMENT CHURCH

The New Testament picks up every one of those Old Testament temple functions and carries them further. In Acts 2, we find they are actually condensed into just a few verses that the rest of the New Testament explains and expands upon. All of God's purposes for the temple—to provide spiritual, healing, material, and relational resources—are found here:

They were continually devoting themselves to the apostles' teaching and to fellowship, to the breaking of bread and to prayer. Everyone kept feeling a sense of awe; and many wonders and signs were taking place through the apostles. And all those who had believed were together and had all things in common; and they began selling their property and possessions and were sharing them with all, as anyone might have need. Day by day continuing with one mind in the temple, and breaking bread from house to house, they were taking their meals together with gladness and sincerity of heart, praising God and having favor with all the people. And the Lord was adding to their number day by day those who were being saved. (Acts 2:42–47)

Spiritual resources. Material resources. Healing resources. Relational resources. God's blueprint for the Old Testament temple became the blueprint for the New Testament church... except the New Testament adds one additional element. The temple now, the place where God chooses to dwell, is no longer inanimate.

And coming to Him as to a living stone which has been rejected by men, but is choice and precious in the sight of God, you also, as living stones, are being built up as a spiritual house for a holy priesthood, to offer up spiritual sacrifices acceptable to God through Jesus Christ. (1 Peter 2:4–5)

Peter continued:

But you are a chosen race, a royal priesthood, a holy nation, a people for God's own possession, so that you may proclaim the excellencies of Him who has called you out of darkness into His marvelous light; for you once were not a people, but now you are the people of God; you had not received mercy, but now you have received mercy. (1 Peter 2:9–10)

The issue of the temple is just as precious to God today as it was in the days of the Old Testament because the temple, the church, remains His chosen instrument to show and give His love in this world. Only the outward form has changed. The temple continues as the visible proclamation of who He is. The difference in the New Testament is that we as a people constitute the structure, the visible proclamation of who He is. Together, we make up the place where He chooses to dwell.

> THE TEMPLE IS JUST AS PRECIOUS TO GOD TODAY.
> THE CHURCH REMAINS HIS CHOSEN INSTRUMENT TO SHOW AND
> GIVE HIS LOVE IN THIS WORLD.

His vision for this temple differs not at all from His vision for the Old Testament temple: that it would provide spiritual resources among us, material resources for caring for people, healing resources, and relational resources.

BACK TO HAGGAI

God saw that those returning from exile in Babylon were poor and miserable and nothing worked for them in their personal lives, so He explained why this was so. They labored in futility because the house of God lay desolate and neglected while they focused on their own homes, their own needs, and their own concerns. They wanted to settle their own personal matters before they would devote themselves to God's communal vision for them—and their way wasn't working.

God has always rejected leftovers, wanting first fruits. What if the only gifts you and I received every Christmas were hand-me-downs? How would we feel? The Babylon returnees tried to justify giving God the leftovers because they believed their own needs had priority over love for God and resources sacrificed for the sake of the whole people. Yet shouldn't the gifts with which we honor God be the first and best?

Haggai's message was that if the people wanted to set things right in their lives and families, to find prosperity, healing, and joy, then they needed to prioritize the temple of the Lord, not just for the sake of blessing God, but for the benefit of all the people.

Remember that list of resources? In New Testament terms, God put us all in this together as *living stones* in a temple called by Him to function just like the physical building in the Old Testament, so all of those resources would be available for all the people.

USING RESOURCES TO BLESS OTHERS

When I pour my resources into the temple—the people of God together—then God pours His resources into my personal life. Recently, my wife and I gave a large sum of money over and above the tithe that we give to our church to enable a family living in a motel to get into a home. As a pastor, I am responsible to withhold my own taxes, including the more than 15 percent for Social Security. We deposit this money into a savings account so we can draw that money out to pay those taxes on schedule four times a year. The gift we gave that family came from this account. It was a risk that set us behind in our savings for our quarterly tax payments.

I'm telling this story not to toot our own horn, but to illustrate that when God promised Israel that if they took care of the temple first, all those resources would be available for all the people and God would be with them. In the weeks after the sacrifice we made for that family, we reaped blessings from God that went far beyond the gift we gave. The risk turned out to be no risk at all.

When Israel turned from self-focus to restore the temple with all of its resources, to benefit the whole people, God said, "I am with you." This is the glory of kingdom economics!

LIVING STONES

No building made of stone can stand if the stones don't stay put. The Holy Spirit holds the temple together with the mortar of relationship in love as we, the stones, sacrifice time and resources, giving of ourselves to be invested in one another. First fruits, not leftovers!

It's a covenant consistency. Jesus taught that our heart will go where our investment lies. Our sense of belonging will go where we've given of ourselves in connection with others. I feel that I belong with the people of my church, not because they're all beautiful, wonderful people who always do and say the right things, but because I've invested sacrificially in them of my time and my resources.

In Haggai's day, God was upset that the temple had not been rebuilt because its absence meant that Israel had no storehouse of resources to care for people. They had no rallying point where relationships and covenant bonds could develop. As a result, love dried up, along with the accompanying sense of belonging. Where there was no love, the manifestation of God's presence could not flow because God *is* love. Until they repented and adjusted their priorities, their plans were not His plans, and so God withdrew His blessing.

> *"You look for much, but behold, it comes to little; when you bring it home, I blow it away. Why?" declares the* Lord *of hosts, "Because of My house which lies desolate, while each of you runs to his own house."*   (Haggai 1:9)

Whether it's the Old Testament physical structure or the New Testament building made of living stones, the house of God cannot lie desolate without God being angry. Why? Because *He loves* and He wants His house to be a place of abundant resources for dispensing and expressing His love. The coming outpouring of God's Spirit will be built upon a restoration of His vision for the temple among a people living a culture of the kingdom of God.

> GOD WANTS HIS HOUSE TO BE A PLACE OF ABUNDANT RESOURCES
> FOR DISPENSING AND EXPRESSING HIS LOVE.

If there are to be material resources in the Lord's house to meet the needs of the poor and if you are one of those poor once in a while, those resources can only come from your faithfulness *now* in making the needs of others more important than your own. If there are to be healing resources in the church, they can only come through the dedication of people who have caught the meaning of the Father's love for us and who are willing to sacrifice to share it, just as Jesus Himself did. This is the Father's love. This is how it all works.

If there are to be relational resources in the church—a place of belonging, love, security, and safety for all who come—then enough of us must value others' needs above our own needs or our own feelings. The last days' outpouring of God's Spirit will be a repudiation of ways of doing church based in the entertainment model in which people come as individuals, listen to three songs expertly performed, hear a nice sermon, and then go home an hour later as individuals. In the New Testament restored temple, there is a concerted sacrifice of praise in worship, room for God to move in sovereignty, healing bodies and hearts, touching lives, and then a commitment to connected fellowship day by day throughout the rest of the week.

Psalm 68:6 says, "*God makes a home for the lonely.*" Be part of something, some kind of smaller group within the larger congregation. In the New Testament temple, no one has to be lonely or feel as if they don't belong. All it takes is an investment in the lives of others and your heart will follow your investment.

Be present for corporate worship and release your spirit into it. Be there for fellowship in a smaller setting for learning and ministry to others. People depend on you. You're a living stone in a spiritual temple with a key role to play. Don't let your part of the wall fall down. Whether you know it or not, others are designed by God to interlink with you—living stones—and you're designed for them. There are stones above you, below you, and beside you. As in any stone structure, removal of even one stone sends cracks through the entire wall of the building.

> ## TOGETHER, INTERLOCKED, WE CONSTITUTE A TEMPLE FOR THE DWELLING OF GOD TO MAKE A DECLARATION TO THE WORLD.

Together, interlocked, we constitute a temple for the dwelling of God to make a declaration to the world. Old Testament and New Testament speak with one voice. God has the same heart now as He did then. God calls us in His love in the same way throughout eternity.

In Haggai's time, the people finally *"obeyed the voice of the* Lord *their God and the words of Haggai the prophet...*[and] *showed reverence for the* Lord. *Then Haggai, the messenger of the* Lord, *spoke by the commission of the* Lord *to the people saying, 'I am with you,' declares the* Lord" (Haggai 1:12–13).

Heeding the Word of the Lord, the people repented, set aside their personal concerns and worries over their own homes, and placed a priority on restoring the Lord's temple so there would be resources there for everyone. Then their prophet shared God's simple yet powerful affirming statement: "*I am with you.*" And the fortunes of a whole people turned for the better.

God has a plan and it's a simple one. Call it *the economy of the kingdom*. It's this: He gives us His love, we freely give love to others, He multiplies His love back to us, and it blesses and releases every aspect of our lives as we become, together, the visible temple able to provide all those resources for all the people.

> THE ECONOMY OF GOD'S KINGDOM IS THIS:
> GOD GIVES US HIS LOVE, WE FREELY GIVE LOVE TO OTHERS,
> AND HE MULTIPLIES HIS LOVE BACK TO US.

It's so basic and clear, although it flies in the face of the culture of self-focus in which we live and by which our churches and our theologies have been so deeply influenced. *Love enough* to give and then experience the love more because you gave. *Love enough* to make His kingdom and the needs of His people more important than your own and then experience more love and more richness *because you loved*.

He will be with you and prosper you. Isaiah 60 will become a reality as we live in the greatest outpouring of God's Spirit since Pentecost, having the time of our lives fulfilling our destiny to influence this world in the midst of a gathering darkness.

Arise, shine; for your light has come, and the glory of the LORD has risen upon you. For behold, darkness will cover the earth and deep darkness the peoples; but the LORD will rise upon you and His glory will appear upon you. Nations will come to your light, and kings to the brightness of your rising. (Isaiah 60:1–3)

2

THE PRESENCE, HEAVEN, AND HOLINESS

John the Baptist came on the scene, announcing that the kingdom of God was imminent and that the Messiah, the promised King of Israel, was at hand. In effect, John proclaimed the coming of a great revival and called people to prepare. Repentance, cleansing, and holiness formed the heart of his message.

Today, we see a similar thing beginning to take shape. As John came in the spirit and power of Elijah to prepare the way, prophetic voices now rise to proclaim that the greatest outpouring of the Holy Spirit in history is coming. The great last days' move of God approaches and the call for preparation now is the same as John preached so long ago. Through reliable prophetic voices, God now cries for holiness and cleansing to uproot everything in ourselves and in our churches not solidly rooted in the nature of Jesus and the Father.

Although dramatic encounters with God certainly occur in times of revival, real revival has never been about having an experience. Real revival sees people transformed into the image of the Son.

> *And we know that God causes all things to work together for good to those who love God, to those who are called according to His purpose. For those whom He foreknew, He also predestined to become conformed to the image of His Son, so that He would be the firstborn among many brethren.*   (Romans 8:28–29)

We have entered a season of salvation history in which there can be no more hidden iniquity. Glory is coming, but the glory sent to bless becomes the pressure that destroys when it rests upon a faulty or cracked foundation. The warning has been issued and we see it in multiple exposures of sin in leadership all over the world. Things we once got away with in the outer court will get us crushed and destroyed in the inner court into which the Holy Spirit now calls us.

> **THE GLORY SENT TO BLESS BECOMES THE PRESSURE THAT DESTROYS WHEN IT RESTS UPON A FAULTY OR CRACKED FOUNDATION.**

Two key words of the hour are the Father's heart—that is, His love that surpasses all understanding—and holiness. These two go hand in hand. Holiness and the heart of the Father require cleansing, which requires repentance. In the original languages of the Bible, holiness means that we have been set apart for God's purposes and we must not allow ourselves to be used for any other purpose. Obviously, this doesn't mean we must all become monks and nuns, but it *does* mean that every aspect of life becomes caught up in His presence to serve the purposes of His glory and love.

FOCUS ON THE CROSS

Every real historic revival sprang from a focus on the cross, the blood, and repentance. Holiness matters. God is about to do something stunning, but the vast majority of the body of Christ is *not* ready, is sound asleep, or is captivated by a culture of self that ultimately fails to serve the purposes of the kingdom of God. Too often and too much, we seek the glory without a focus on the cross where we die to self with Him, the blood that cleanses, and the resurrection that releases life. We seek experiences of His touch, but fail to share in His self-sacrificial death. Because we fail to share in His death, we cannot attain resurrection life.

Worship then becomes a show. Church services become fluffy pats on the back that tell us how good we are, or how to be healthy, wealthy, and wise without truly changing the lives of those who attend. Revival becomes an effort to fill the seats rather than make passionate disciples.

The gospel of self-improvement can *never* be the gospel of God. It can never make good on what it promises. All real Christianity flows to and from the cross. The apostle Paul wrote:

> I have been crucified with Christ; and it is no longer I who live, but Christ lives in me; and the life which I now live in the flesh I live by faith in the Son of God, who loved me and gave Himself up for me.   (Galatians 2:20)

Therein lies the heart of our life as Christians.

CLEANSING IMPURITY

I was always taught that because God couldn't tolerate impurity in His presence, He had to sacrifice Jesus to pay for our sin and clothe us with His righteousness, as if somehow God's intolerance or allergy to sin forced Him to send Jesus to die. The message seemed to be that He loves us with His nose plugged and can't come near us without the sacrifice of Jesus to apply some serious deodorant to our malodorous condition.

That picture, however, fails to present Him as the purely and entirely loving Father revealed to us by Jesus. (See, for example, John 17:23.) It pictures Him rather as a petty, judgmental figure, a Father who is so angry with the children He claims to love that He cries, "Get out of my sight, I can't stand to look at you!" The Father we learned about from Jesus never disowns His sons and daughters for failure. The god of the Pharisees (small "g" intended) did that, but not the Father whom Jesus came to reveal.

Regardless of how some seem to view the Old Testament Scriptures, this picture of God with His nose plugged utterly fails to reflect God as we actually see Him, even in the Old Testament before Jesus came. God's love and mercy kept David as king and as a man after His own heart, even after David committed adultery with Bathsheba and had her husband killed. Our Father God forgave Abraham's failures of faith, not only loving him through those failures and remaining close to him, but also calling him a friend and the forerunner of righteousness by faith. Remember that Abraham gave his wife into a foreign king's harem in order to preserve his own life and yet God launched a holy nation out of his loins that ultimately brought forth Jesus.

> GOD NEVER CHANGES, SO WE MUST READ AND UNDERSTAND OLD TESTAMENT THINGS THROUGH THE LENS OF THE NEW TESTAMENT AND THE REVELATION OF JESUS.

Because God never changes, we must read and understand Old Testament things through the lens of the New Testament and the revelation of Jesus, knowing that the Old Testament remains the eternal Word of God.

FELLOWSHIP AND INTIMACY WITH GOD

God longs for fellowship and intimacy with us; He is hurt that we, created in His image, have been cut off from Him by sin, brokenness, and defilement. The distance exists, but it's not because He can't tolerate the unholy. He's bigger than that. Unlike me, God doesn't throw up when He changes a messy diaper.

> GOD LONGS FOR FELLOWSHIP AND INTIMACY WITH US, BUT IN OUR SINFUL, BROKEN STATE, HIS GLORY WOULD DESTROY US.

The truth is that in our unprotected, broken, and sinful state, if we were exposed to the raw, unfiltered glory and goodness of God, it would destroy us—and that would be neither God's fault nor His will. He is what He is, never changing. The reality is that His radiant holiness, compassion, tenderness, love, and power are so pure that we could never survive the fullness of His glory in our wickedness and shame. It would destroy us. Not His fault. Not His attitude. It's us.

Longing for intimacy with us, therefore, Jesus died as the sacrifice for our sin, to cleanse us and enable us to enter into the raw, radiant presence and glory of the Father, wearing the righteousness of Jesus, clean and safe. This is why He said, *"I am the way, and the truth, and the life; no one comes to the Father but through Me"* (John 14:6). The apostle Paul wrote, *"He made Him who knew no sin to be sin on our behalf, so that we might become the righteousness of God in Him"* (2 Corinthians 5:21).

God has made no other provision to enable us to enter His raw presence and survive. Only Jesus's sacrifice on our behalf, cleansing and covering us, makes that possible. Heaven and how we get there have nothing to do with God being so merciful and kind that He could never send anyone to hell. Neither does it have anything to do with any of us being good enough to merit heaven on our own.

Cheap grace and universalism have become popular in our day, but these things completely miss the reality. In order for there to be a heaven, there must be a hell. First, if the unrepentant and uncleansed were allowed to enter heaven, they would rapidly turn it into the hell they created on earth. Second, too many fail to realize the effect of the holy upon the unholy. Those not clothed with the holiness of Jesus—paid for at the cross and imparted to us—would be destroyed by His holiness. This would be neither God's fault nor His will, any more than it would be the will of the sun to destroy the Starship Enterprise if it was flown into the sun without some kind of heat shield.

We can feel the warmth of the sun at a distance. It feels good and gives life. We would die without it, but if we were to fly too close, it would kill us, not because the sun is evil, but because the sun is what it is. The sun is a beautiful and radiant thing; gazing into it without protection causes blindness.

> JESUS SACRIFICED HIMSELF IN ORDER TO CLEANSE SIN AND CLOTHE US WITH HIS OWN RIGHTEOUSNESS.

Similarly, we can sense the warmth and goodness of God at a distance, seeing and feeling His light, but we cannot enter the raw, immediate, unveiled, and unfiltered fullness of His presence without the protection provided to us through the cross and resurrection of Jesus. Without those, we would be destroyed. Jesus sacrificed Himself in order to cleanse sin and clothe us with His own righteousness. In heaven, and even here on earth, we can safely enter and enjoy the fullness of the radiance and power of God as we wear what Jesus has given us: salvation by grace through faith, not of our own works, but by what Jesus has done for us.

HISTORY, THE GLORY, AND MANKIND

ADAM AND EVE

God doesn't change. He cannot alter who and what He Himself is, but He *can* change *us*. He therefore acted to transform us through Jesus.

Our story began in the Garden of Eden with the first couple, Adam and Eve. They walked in God's raw presence unguarded and unshielded, whole and pure. Nothing stood between them and God. And then sin entered in.

When they ate from the Tree of Knowledge of Good and Evil, they brought death and defilement into the world. Wickedness and destruction began to multiply. What had been perfect became defiled and broken. They could no longer walk in the place of exposed and vulnerable intimacy with God, not because God was angry, but because their brokenness made it dangerous. The purely holy destroys the unholy. Having eaten from the forbidden tree, they had become unholy. Not to punish them, but for their own protection, God expelled Adam and Eve from the garden where they had walked naked with God. Punishment by itself serves no redemptive purpose. God's discipline redeems and preserves. God is love. He never changes.

Then the LORD God said, "Behold, the man has become like one of Us, knowing good and evil; and now, he might stretch

out his hand, and take also from the tree of life, and eat, and
live forever"—therefore the LORD *God sent him out from*
the garden of Eden, to cultivate the ground from which he
was taken. So He drove the man out; and at the east of the
garden of Eden He stationed the cherubim and the flaming
sword which turned every direction to guard the way to the
tree of life.   (Genesis 3:22–24)

In light of New Testament revelation of the true nature of Father God, I think the angel and the sword guarding the way to the Tree of Life were more for protection than for penalty. Although it might seem like a punishment, consider what might have happened if Adam and Eve, in their defiled state, had lived forever and remained in the intimacy of direct access to God's raw presence? In their brokenness and defilement, it would have destroyed and tortured them through an undying eternity.

The heart of a loving Father spared them that, although, as it was, Adam and Eve had to hide from God and wear fig leaves to cover their nakedness and vulnerability because walking uncovered in the unveiled presence of God was no longer safe. The certainty of death, pain in childbirth, and hard labor to make the earth produce were penalty enough. God wanted them to live.

MOSES AND THE GLORY

Much later, Moses fled Egypt after killing the taskmaster he saw beating a Hebrew slave. Forty years passed before he encountered God in a burning bush that wasn't consumed. In the New Testament, Stephen told the story best, just before being stoned to death for his faith:

After forty years had passed, an angel appeared to him in
the wilderness of Mount Sinai, in the flame of a burning

thorn bush. When Moses saw it, he marveled at the sight; and as he approached to look more closely, there came the voice of the Lord: "I am the God of your fathers, the God of Abraham and Isaac and Jacob." Moses shook with fear and would not venture to look. But the Lord said to him, "Take off the sandals from your feet, for the place on which you are standing is holy ground." (Acts 7:30–33)

Why the fear? And why remove his shoes for the sake of holy ground? Moses saw only a filtered vision of the Lord; His glory was veiled, yet unmasked sufficiently to endanger Moses in his uncleanness and fill him with fear. In the culture of the day, feet were considered defiling. His footwear was dirty. Impurity would have put him at risk in the pure and raw presence of the Lord. Removing the impurity of his shoes therefore protected him from harm while he stood so near the perfect holiness of God, shielded as the revelation was.

In Exodus 19, the people have left Egypt and have come to Mount Sinai, where Moses is to receive the Law from God.

The LORD came down on Mount Sinai, to the top of the mountain; and the LORD called Moses to the top of the mountain, and Moses went up. Then the LORD spoke to Moses, "Go down, warn the people, so that they do not break through to the LORD to gaze, and many of them perish. Also let the priests who come near to the LORD consecrate themselves, or else the LORD will break out against them." Moses said to the LORD, "The people cannot come up to Mount Sinai, for You warned us, saying, 'Set bounds about the mountain and consecrate it.'" Then the LORD said to him, "Go down and come up again, you and Aaron with you; but do not let the priests and the people break through to come up to the LORD, *or He will break forth upon them."*   (Exodus 19:20–24)

Keep in mind that *God is love* and desperately longs to be with us. So why would He tell Moses to keep the people away from Him? In love, God wanted to protect them from harm. In love, He called them out of slavery and passed them through the Red Sea with the walls of water standing up on either side to protect them from Pharaoh's pursuing army. The one thing God cannot do is change who and what He is. In the people's unholy and broken state, His raw presence and perfect holiness would have destroyed them. As an act of love, He therefore set up protections to keep them at a safe distance.

> ## THE ONE THING GOD CANNOT DO IS CHANGE WHO AND WHAT HE IS.

The Lord told Moses to establish the priesthood and the tent of meeting. The priests had to be perfect, wearing certain clothing and bearing no physical flaws.

> *You shall make for them linen breeches to cover their bare flesh; they shall reach from the loins even to the thighs. They shall be on Aaron and on his sons when they enter the tent of meeting, or when they approach the altar to minister in the holy place, so that they do not incur guilt and die. It shall be a statute forever to him and to his descendants after him.*   (Exodus 28:42–43)

The priests' impurity would have destroyed them in the unfiltered presence of God—and it would not have been God's fault. God had no fear of defilement. He feared, rather, for the safety of those who would approach Him. God is who He is.

To enable them to approach His glory safely, the God of love provided filters and shields. Love provides for that.

DAVID AND UZZAH

David had taken Jerusalem and established it as his capital. Full of excitement and love for the Lord, he was determined to bring the ark of the covenant, the very throne of God, into the city.

> *They placed the ark of God on a new cart that they might bring it from the house of Abinadab which was on the hill; and Uzzah and Ahio, the sons of Abinadab, were leading the new cart. So they brought it with the ark of God from the house of Abinadab, which was on the hill; and Ahio was walking ahead of the ark. Meanwhile, David and all the house of Israel were celebrating before the LORD with all kinds of instruments made of fir wood, and with lyres, harps, tambourines, castanets and cymbals. But when they came to the threshing floor of Nacon, Uzzah reached out toward the ark of God and took hold of it, for the oxen nearly upset it. And the anger of the LORD burned against Uzzah, and God struck him down there for his irreverence; and he died there by the ark of God.*   (2 Samuel 6:3–7)

There were protocols and procedures for handling the ark that God designed to protect those who would approach it. Uzzah impulsively failed to adhere to these, so the impact of God's unfiltered purity, power, and raw presence killed him.

What about the anger of God that broke forth? Did that seem fair? How could a loving God be angry because someone with the best intentions touched the ark improperly? Why was God angry with Uzzah's irreverence? God instituted protocols for approaching Him in order to ensure the safety of those who did so. In Uzzah's case, these were violated. Was God motivated by vanity and pettiness? Obviously not. God puts protocols in place for our protection, as an expression of His love.

> GOD PUTS PROTOCOLS IN PLACE FOR OUR PROTECTION,
> AS AN EXPRESSION OF HIS LOVE.

We often do the same thing. For example, in the 1980s, my family and I lived in Idaho, where winters can be very cold. We heated our home with a wood stove. Would the child who touched the hot stove get burned? Would a parent be angry with a child who had been warned repeatedly not to touch the hot stove? Yes to both questions...but parental anger over such a transgression would be an expression of love for the child's sake, even as the parent would feel compassion for the child's pain. God's anger is often parental anger born of love for His children.

God establishes rules and protocols to protect us broken sinners from the effect of the raw presence of God in our unclean state. Uzzah got burned, not because God is some kind of angry judge enforcing meaningless rules, but because people can be hurt by His raw presence when unprepared to enter it. The life-giving warmth of the sun can be felt at a distance, but with too much exposure, it can kill. In small doses, exposure to the sun stimulates our bodies to produce vitamin D, but long exposure without sunscreen can do serious damage. In the same away that the sun cannot change its nature, neither can God. He is who and what He is.

ISAIAH'S ENCOUNTER

In Isaiah 6, we see Isaiah standing before the heavenly throne. Seraphim fly around the throne crying, "Holy, holy, holy!" while the voice of God causes the ground to shake and the heavenly temple fills with smoke. A modern-day Christian filled with a mushy picture of the Great Teddy Bear in the Sky might respond with some version of, "Isn't this wonderful!? I just feel so comfortable in my Lord's presence! I feel so uplifted by the worship service!"

In contrast, Isaiah's response was: *"Woe is me, for I am ruined! Because I am a man of unclean lips, and I live among a people of unclean lips; for my eyes have seen the King, the LORD of hosts"* (Isaiah 6:5). In the next two verses, we read the remedy for his pain.

> *Then one of the seraphim flew to me with a burning coal in his hand, which he had taken from the altar with tongs. He touched my mouth with it and said, "Behold, this has touched your lips; and your iniquity is taken away and your sin is forgiven."* (Isaiah 6:6–7)

With his sin burned away for the moment, Isaiah could safely stand in the place of the Lord's presence and power to receive His prophetic commission. Until that coal touched his lips, Isaiah was affected and hurt by the raw presence of God touching his uncleanness. God wasn't torturing him. Rather, his own brokenness and sin reacted to God's raw power and presence.

PAIN OF THE PRESENCE IN REVELATION

> *Then the kings of the earth and the great men and the commanders and the rich and the strong and every slave and free man hid themselves in the caves and among the rocks of the mountains; and they said to the mountains and to the rocks, "Fall on us and hide us from the presence of Him who sits on the throne, and from the wrath of the Lamb; for*

> *the great day of their wrath has come, and who is able to*
> *stand?"*   (Revelation 6:15–17)

In Revelation, when Jesus appears in the fullness of His unfiltered glory, unbelievers—those who have not been clothed in the gift of Jesus's righteousness won at the cross—cry out to be hidden from His presence. It's painful and terrifying for them. It's not that Jesus's presence is bad or that He wants to hurt anyone. In these verses Jesus is not willfully torturing them. His presence and the revelation of all that He is remains good, filled with love and power, but when His glory is unveiled, their uncleansed sin can't tolerate it.

THE GOOD NEWS

> *Husbands, love your wives, just as Christ also loved the*
> *church and gave Himself up for her, so that He might sanc-*
> *tify her, having cleansed her by the washing of water with*
> *the word, that He might present to Himself the church in all*
> *her glory, having no spot or wrinkle or any such thing; but*
> *that she would be holy and blameless.*
>   (Ephesians 5:25–27)

JESUS CLEANSES HIS BRIDE, THE CHURCH,
IN LOVE BY LAYING HIS LIFE DOWN FOR HER.

If you're wondering how these verses apply to the subject at hand, understand that Jesus presents the church to Himself and safely gathers her in as a bride. However, He first cleanses her in love by laying His life down for her. Because of His cleansing sacrifice, we can come into His intimate presence and be blessed by it rather than destroyed. Jesus made it possible for us to know and truly experience the love that passes understanding.

HOLINESS *STILL* MATTERS

I charge you in the presence of God, who gives life to all things, and of Christ Jesus, who testified the good confession before Pontius Pilate, that you keep the commandment without stain or reproach until the appearing of our Lord Jesus Christ, which He will bring about at the proper time—He who is the blessed and only Sovereign, the King of kings and Lord of lords, who alone possesses immortality and dwells in unapproachable light. (1 Timothy 6:13–16)

Why did Paul write that exhortation to holiness to a New Testament Christian covered by the blood of Jesus and walking in the righteousness given to him by the gift of grace through the cross? Because holiness still matters, even in New Testament times, as we walk under grace, carrying in and with us the righteousness of Jesus. We cannot save ourselves by our own goodness, but only through His. Note the phrase *"unapproachable light."* Only in Him can this change so that we can, indeed, approach the light.

Paul wrote this warning to Timothy because unholiness and compromise can still hinder us from experiencing the fullness of the presence of God. Sin can still form a barrier between us. God does not erect the barrier; we ourselves do. Holy and unholy cannot mix. In this way, we still reap for the sin we sow, even though it's forgiven.

The apostle Paul wrote, *"Do not be deceived, God is not mocked; for whatever a man sows, this he will also reap. For the one who sows to his own flesh will from the flesh reap corruption, but the one who sows to the Spirit will from the Spirit reap eternal life"* (Galatians 6:7–8). Even under the new covenant, we suffer the consequences of our compromises and sins. The cross does not negate that. It only opens the way to forgiveness, cleansing, and, ultimately, heaven.

> **THE CROSS DOES NOT NEGATE THE CONSEQUENCES OF OUR COMPROMISES AND SINS.**

For example, you might be a forgiven Christian, but if you commit adultery, you're going to have a problem in your marriage. That problem will, in turn, affect your relationship with God. You might be a forgiven Christian, but if you use drugs to get high, you're going to have to live with the hangover, or the jail time if you drive, or the damage you've just done to your spirit, as well as the difficulty it will create for you where hearing and sensing God are concerned.

Grace means that God uses the consequences of our sin to change, cleanse, and refine us, but we reap nevertheless. Personally, I'd rather avoid that. On the other hand, if you're not in Him, cleansed, forgiven, and walking in His grace, then the reaping simply destroys.

Sometimes I wonder if God doesn't withhold or filter out a bit of the glory for our sake, knowing that the weight of His glory on a faulty foundation would do us harm, notwithstanding His sacrifice and the gift of His righteousness upon us. I find this to be true especially when we're off-base, or walking as a people in something that isn't right or whole. You can only safely carry as much as your inner wholeness will bear.

How can we expect to experience and minister the pure love and healing power of God if we carry defilement in our lives, or if we are broken up inside by judgments, bitterness, anger, or compromise? How can we expect to experience the fullness of His presence if we've traded our sexual glory for the defilement of fornication, pornography, and adultery? How can we expect to be bathed in His love when we've betrayed or abandoned our brothers and sisters by absenting ourselves from fellowship and corporate worship?

Holiness matters in these last days. Faithfulness matters. Righteousness matters. Morality matters. Integrity matters. We have a world to reach, as well as personal glory to enjoy and walk in.

ONENESS AS A HOLINESS ISSUE

Unity in the body of Christ matters. This, too, is a holiness issue. It's long past time that we in the body of Christ honored the prayer of Jesus in John 17:

> *For their sakes I sanctify Myself, that they themselves also may be sanctified in truth. I do not ask on behalf of these alone, but for those also who believe in Me through their word; that they may all be one; even as You, Father, are in Me and I in You, that they also may be in Us, so that the world may believe that You sent Me. The glory which You have given Me I have given to them, that they may be one, just as We are one; I in them and You in Me, that they may be perfected in unity, so that the world may know that You sent Me, and loved them, even as You have loved Me.*
> (John 17:19–23)

I don't see how we, as a body of believers, could stand in the presence of God in fullness while walking in a divided state. Worshiping with one heart and spirit, hearing the Word with one heart and spirit, and loving one another with one mind—all lead to releases of power and glory. As the heart of holiness, these things matter. There can be no excuse, no holy reason, for ongoing division.

IMPOSSIBILITIES AND THE REMEDY

It remains impossible to come fully into the presence of the Lord in an unholy state that has not been surrendered to Jesus. We can feel the warmth and see the occasional miracle, but the fullness comes only with purity and holiness. God doesn't change. It's not Him handing down destruction when we allow unholiness into our lives, or when we continue to walk in brokenness. It's simply the effect of His purity and the undimmed love and light of God shining on what is not holy. It's not that God can't tolerate the unholy. It's that the unholy can't tolerate the holy and would actually be damaged by it.

Many years ago, I built English sports cars as a hobby. Early on, I learned that I could restore every system on the car and make it look new, but if the fuel filter was clogged, the car would be powerless.

Is our fuel system clogged? If the fullness of power and love seem to be blocked, then what dirt has gotten into the fuel line?

The good news is that God gave us a remedy: the cross of Jesus Christ, the emblem of selflessness. As the apostle Paul said, *"I have been crucified with Christ; and it is no longer I who live, but Christ lives in me; and the life which I now live in the flesh I live by faith in the Son of God, who loved me and gave Himself up for me"* (Galatians 2:20). There lies the heart of our holiness. There we find the answer to entering the raw presence of God. There we find the gift of a loving Father who longs for intimacy with His kids.

3

THE KINGDOM IS AT HAND

In a prayer meeting in November 2019, the Lord quickened me to review Isaiah 7:10–13, written at a time when King Ahaz of Israel had just weathered a siege of Jerusalem. God spoke to him through Isaiah: *"Then the LORD spoke again to Ahaz, saying, 'Ask a sign for yourself from the LORD your God; make it deep as Sheol or high as heaven.' But Ahaz said, 'I will not ask, nor will I test the LORD!' Then [Isaiah] said, 'Listen now, O house of David! Is it too slight a thing for you to try the patience of men, that you will try the patience of my God as well?'"*

Through Isaiah, God told King Ahaz to make an outrageous request with no limit, saying in essence, "Go beyond what you believe can happen, beyond what you can actually see, or what you feel you can reach—deep as the depths of Sheol, the place of the dead, or as high as heaven." When Ahaz refused, for lack of faith or too small a vision, both Isaiah and the Lord responded with frustrated anger, saying in effect, "You're trying my patience!"

In other words, God was saying through Isaiah, "I have worked with you. I have fed you. I have been faithful to you. You have been attacked by enemies, but I have prevented your enemies from breaching the walls of the city and destroying you. You know who I am. So, on the basis of what I have done for you in saving you and your city from your enemies, now I tell you to ask for the greater thing, more than you can see or understand, without limit, but you refuse to do it. And your excuse for your unbelief sounds so religious. 'I won't test the Lord.' What a load of nonsense, Ahaz! You won't test Me with what I ask you to test Me with, but you *will* choose to test My patience!"

In that prayer time in November, I prayed, "Lord, if this is what You're speaking now, then what shall I ask? I don't want to be silly or frivolous." I knew for certain that the Lord wasn't talking about several million dollars for a new building, or a best-selling book, or an eighty-inch flat-screen, 4k HDR TV.

What the Lord actually poured into me is that so many of us have been praying for revival—and we've been wrong. Our concept of what revival looks like is too little and too limited. Many of us have felt ourselves under siege, like Ahaz, and God has preserved us within our walls, but it has caused our vision to shrivel up. Our thinking is too small.

WE NEED A MOVEMENT

We don't need what we've thought of as revival. *What we need is a movement.* Revival is life from death and waking from slumber; it's for people who are already Christian. *A movement is like a tsunami wave* that sweeps everything before it. It can't be contained by the walls of the church or held within the confines of those who are already Christian. You can erect barriers or thick walls before a tsunami, but the wave will destroy them in a moment. It washes away everything it touches and carries everything to different places. It can't be resisted. The tsunami is not like surfing, where you can choose your wave and ride it with skill while you remain basically in control. That's revival. In a tsunami movement, you're out of control. You're swept away.

> WE NEED A TSUNAMI MOVEMENT THAT WE CANNOT CONTROL, THAT SWEEPS US AWAY.

We have not seen a real movement in the Christian world since the early 1970s. The Jesus Movement caught fire just as I entered adulthood and it was a tsunami that swept hundreds of thousands of young people into the kingdom of God. You didn't have to work with people for weeks on end to get them to come to Jesus. You could stand on a street corner and shout "Jesus" and people would get saved. It became a culturally cool thing to belong to Jesus.

We had speed freaks and we had Jesus freaks. I'll never forget going to a rock festival at Farragut State Park in north Idaho in 1970 or '71. I stood on top of a hill and looked down into the natural amphitheater below, where the music was blasting and where people were dancing naked in the dust. But the words to the song I heard wafting up from below were, "Well hurray for the Jesus people! At least they know just where they're at."

In California, people were baptized in the ocean by the thousands. Signs and wonders followed. Lives were changed in a moment. You didn't have to counsel people for months on end to repair their damaged lives after they came. Yes, we counseled people because it was needed, but healing and transformation came a lot faster. Talk about acceleration! In a movement, everything moves more quickly. People got delivered in a blinding instant and never went back. That's a movement.

The Vineyard was a wonderful renewal, but it wasn't really a movement. It renewed the people of God and it had an evangelistic thrust, but it didn't sweep through a generation like a tsunami. The Toronto Blessing was a renewal, an important one, but not a movement. Again, there was a heart for winning souls, but it didn't spawn a sweeping movement. The Brownsville/Pensacola Revival was a renewal that confronted people with holiness and repentance. God moved, but it wasn't a movement. Bethel Church in Redding, California, is a renewal for the church, once again with a heart for winning souls, but it's not a movement like we saw with the Jesus Movement.

> ## A MOVEMENT RUSHES OVER THOSE OUTSIDE THE CHURCH AND SWEEPS THEM IN.

A movement touches more than the church internally, the already saved. It rushes over those outside the church and sweeps them in. You don't have to labor for every soul won. It doesn't take months of laborious counseling to radically change lives because waves of people are caught up in a flow that comes with a level of power so pervasive that masses of people just get swept up in it. It isn't just about sweeping people into church. It touches homes and relationships. People find each other and connect in love. Nothing heals relationships faster than a shared hunger for God.

During the Jesus Movement, a generation of desperate parents saw their children come home to Jesus, restored, washed clean, set on paths to lives that would be productive, swept in by a wave that touched a generation. Out of the Jesus Movement came the old song, "We Are One in the Spirit"[1]:

> We are one in the Spirit,
> We are one in the Lord.
> And we pray that all unity may one day be restored.
> And they'll know we are Christians by our love,
> By our love,
> Yes they'll know we are Christians by our love.

Songs today tend to be more self-centered—heal me, touch me, love me.... Back then, relationships were being made and relationships were being restored. In a tsunami move of the Spirit, you're no longer focused on measuring each other and tallying every failure. Your faces and your hearts are turned toward Him, where the glory of His goodness transforms you.

If God hadn't sent a Jesus Movement in the early '70s, there would be virtually no church in America today. The older generation would have died off and, if we hadn't come to Jesus during those golden years, there would have been too few to replace them. Churches would be standing empty and Christianity would be dead. Today, just like then, we need a movement and we need it now.

THE SEASON TO PREPARE

In the first week of December 2016, just after the 2016 presidential election, in an intercessory prayer meeting held in our sanctuary, I saw four sticks in a vision, with the fourth one bending. I asked the Lord what it meant and He said, "You have four years to prepare." I knew that the bending stick, the fourth year, would be a year of trouble. As I write these words, we find

---

1. Peter Scholtes; © 1966 F.E.L. Church Publications, Ltd. Assigned 1991 to Lorenz Publishing Company.

ourselves in that fourth year, facing a move to impeach the president and an election cycle gathering momentum that promises to be filled with more hate than we usually see.

Impeachment has failed. Barring some form of disaster, the president will be re-elected. Riots and violence will follow as the left erupts in renewed hatred and frustration. The nation is being torn apart by naked hatred—philosophical, racial, ethnic, and generational. Shootings in schools, workplaces, and public places are simply manifestations of the underlying buildup of vileness.

Worse, we find ourselves in the midst of an unprecedented crisis brought on by the coronavirus panic. The world economy has been shut down. Tens of millions in the United States are out of work. Unemployment has reached levels unseen since the Great Depression. Businesses are failing and churches are forbidden to meet.

We need to keep praying and the root of our prayers needs to be a corporate repentance for the sin of our nation, primarily for losing the fear of God, for forgetting who our God really is. The closures of schools and businesses was really a demonically fueled panic. If God's people will stand together, we can transform this nation.

> GOD WILL SEND ANOTHER TSUNAMI MOVEMENT OF HIS SPIRIT
> TO SWEEP MANY THOUSANDS INTO THE KINGDOM—
> BUT WE MUST PREPARE FOR IT.

God is about to send a tsunami of His Spirit, a movement in the midst of gathering darkness. In that sense, history will repeat itself just as the Jesus Movement came when the nation was so divided in the late 1960s and early '70s. In the midst of the turmoil of those days, God sent the Jesus Movement. In the same way, in the midst of the turmoil of the present day, God will send another tsunami movement of His Spirit to sweep many thousands into the kingdom—but we must prepare for it.

I say these things having lived through the Vietnam era and the cultural upheaval that happened then. In 1968, young people rioted at the Democratic National Convention. We saw violence in the streets and anti-war protests. This is a more crucial period of time than that. What we saw back then was youthful rebellion. *This is pure hatred*—very different! I have said for almost the last ten years that we are living on borrowed time and that the days are urgent. Recent years have been a season of grace and favor for us who believe, a time in which to get ready, not just for the turmoil and trouble to come, but to receive and be stewards of the movement God wants to send. The four years I saw in 2016 correspond to Trump's term in office, a time when we have had an administration favorable to the church and Israel, opposed to abortion, and pursuing policies that produced a period of economic prosperity. Four years of grace.

> ## THE TURMOIL AROUND US IS DESIGNED TO LULL US TO SLEEP AND RENDER US INEFFECTIVE.

I've said that the season of grace and lessened pressure on Christians in this nation can be extended by prayer if we wake up to the urgency and shake off the false messages of easy grace, compromised Christianity, and other pollutions and distractions. The turmoil around us is designed to lull us to sleep, to render us ineffective at a time when God is about to pour out His Spirit in unprecedented ways. I have long prophesied that the end time outpouring of the Spirit will be greater than Pentecost, greater and more powerful than anything history has seen. It will be a movement, more than mere revival. With the gathering darkness comes a corresponding outpouring of the Spirit of God and the shining of His presence upon those who have made the choices to follow at any cost.

> *Arise, shine; for your light has come, and the glory of the* LORD *has risen upon you. For behold, darkness will cover the earth and deep darkness the peoples; but the* LORD *will rise upon you and His glory will appear upon you. Nations will come to your light, and kings to the brightness of your rising. Lift up your eyes round about and see; they all gather together, they come to you. Your sons will come from afar, and your daughters will be carried in the arms. Then you will see and be radiant, and your heart will thrill and rejoice; because the abundance of the sea will be turned to you, the wealth of the nations will come to you.*   (Isaiah 60:1–5)

When God is about to do something huge, He consistently sends forerunners to preach preparedness as John the Baptist did to prepare the way for Jesus. His message was, *"Repent, for the kingdom of heaven is at hand"* (Matthew 3:2), as foretold by Isaiah the prophet when he said, *"The voice of one crying in the wilderness, 'Make ready the way of the Lord, make His paths straight!'"* (Matthew 3:3). In the spirit of John the Baptist, the message of preparation never changes in its essence. There needs to be a clear and clean pathway, a place for the coming move of God to land, a foundation on which to rest, a road for Him to travel on.

JOHN THE BAPTIST PROPHETS

A movement of John the Baptist prophets now emerges to prepare the way. They cry for repentance and holiness: "Prepare the way of the Lord!" Although it involves the usual calls for foundational morality, it goes much deeper than that.

For the word of God is living and active and sharper than any two-edged sword, and piercing as far as the division of soul and spirit, of both joints and marrow, and able to judge the thoughts and intentions of the heart. (Hebrews 4:12)

The Word of God penetrates to a revealing and cleansing of everything that fails to conform to the image of Jesus, from the core of ourselves to the expression of it in life. It's a deep, sweet penetration of the Spirit of God that purifies motivations, intentions, ambitions, judgments, and unholy thoughts and attitudes—everything that doesn't reflect Jesus.

The goal is that we shine with the Spirit of God in such a pure way from the depths of ourselves that our very presence becomes a magnet, a testimony, and a visible sign of the goodness of God to anyone who comes near us. *"Nations will come to your light, and kings to the brightness of your rising"* (Isaiah 60:3).

> **THE MESSAGE OF PREPARATION CALLS FOR A SHIFT FROM A FOCUS ON GIFTS OF THE SPIRIT TO THE TRUE SPIRIT OF LOVE.**

The message of preparation calls for a shift from a focus on gifts of the Spirit, performances, and displays to the true Spirit of love who captivates every thought and every inclination of the heart for purity. *Wake up and get ready.*

These John the Baptist prophets have a second preparatory emphasis on prayer. Another thing I've prophesied for at least the last nine years is that we are living literally in the days of Revelation 8.

When the Lamb broke the seventh seal, there was silence in heaven for about half an hour. And I saw the seven angels who stand before God, and seven trumpets were given to them. Another angel came and stood at the altar, holding a golden censer; and much incense was given to him, so that he might add it to the prayers of all the saints on the golden altar which was before the throne. And the smoke of the incense, with the prayers of the saints, went up before God out of the angel's hand. Then the angel took the censer and filled it with the fire of the altar, and threw it to the earth; and there followed peals of thunder and sounds and flashes of lightning and an earthquake. (Revelation 8:1–5)

For more than nine years, I've proclaimed this, while my sense of urgency and timeliness has only grown stronger. Our prayers in this season, as we live literally on the threshold of the events leading to the return of the Lord, are magnified in heaven, mixed with the smoke from that altar of incense in heaven. The angel responds by casting fire into the earth. An earthquake results. Think of *earthquake* as another metaphor for a tsunami wave, a movement of God's Spirit.

In an earthquake, as in a tsunami, you're stuck. You can't hide. You can't escape. You can't control it. That illustrates the power of a movement. The Jesus Movement came in response to the desperate prayers of a generation of parents who were watching their children become lost in drugs and immorality. *The next tsunami move of the Spirit will come in the same way in response to prayer.*

DECLARING AND DECREEING

There comes a time, however, when we must move from praying like beggars for God to come do something for us and enter into a time of declaring and decreeing what He is doing and is going to do as He has revealed it to us. The time has come for genuine prophetic people to assume their posts in the church to guide God's people in their praying, to lead them to pray and decree the will of heaven on earth as it is revealed through the prophetic word. It's time to do it boldly, loudly, aggressively, and with power and authority.

> WE MUST SEEK GOD, HEAR FROM HIM CONCERNING HIS WILL, AND THEN DECREE WITH OUR MOUTHS HIS PURPOSES TO BE ACCOMPLISHED ON EARTH.

Elijah decreed that there would be no rain in Israel unless at his word. (See 1 Kings 17:1.) He could do so because he was decreeing on earth what God had already decreed in heaven— and it happened. I would suggest that we have moved past a time of merely making requests of God for a move of the Spirit for our churches and our nations. No longer do we simply petition God concerning the political turmoil and violence we see escalating. We have come into a time when we must seek God, hear from Him concerning His will, and then decree with our mouths His purposes to be accomplished on earth. To fail to make this move is to fall from acting as sons and daughters of the living God to behaving as beggars before the throne. Isaiah 60:1 says, *"Arise, shine; for your light has come."* That day is now.

THE CALL TO REPENTANCE AND HOPE

The true John the Baptist forerunners proclaim the coming of the King, our Messiah. They announce the move of the Spirit, but they call for the kind of repentance that removes boulders and blockages from the Lord's road to prepare for His coming. In this kind of purity, Jesus is manifested to the world. It's a time to seek wholeness, a time for the depths of us to be transformed to the image of Jesus. It's a time for us to become a sweet aroma to the world around us and a delight to our God. *"Search me, O God, and know my heart; try me and know my anxious thoughts;*

and see if there be any hurtful way in me, and lead me in the ever-lasting way" (Psalm 139:23–24).

Many of us face some difficult life situations and huge challenges. Hopes have been deferred. Disappointments have mounted. Some struggle with betrayals by people they once loved and trusted. There have been marriage problems and problems with children who seem lost to the Lord. Many are burdened by these things, together with financial challenges, fears, and even senses of depression. I get it. I understand because I've walked that path.

These things can put you to sleep and make you incapable of receiving because you block out what God would send. They can weigh you down, sap your strength, erode faith, and create a mindset that just doesn't want to trust or hope again. And then someone like me, a John the Baptist prophetic type, seeks to pump you up, to tell you yet again that God wants to do something unprecedented, that we need to prepare, and God is calling us to, *"Ask a sign for yourself from the* LORD *your God; make it deep as Sheol or high as heaven"* (Isaiah 7:11).

Maybe you're receiving and are already pumped up. Maybe you're struggling to hope again and believe the prophetic word of hope you hear spoken. Either way, when the voice of John the Baptist cries out, when the John the Baptist forerunners lift up their voices to call you to hope, pray, and make what seem to be outrageously impossible requests of the Lord, you must choose to gird up your loins, pack your bags, and go out to the wilderness to get it right with God.

In John the Baptist's day, there hadn't been a move of God in four hundred years. Israel had suffered under Roman occupation, humiliated and oppressed. Religion had become dead legalism. The people had lost real hope. But when John appeared and declared that the kingdom of God was at hand, calling for repentance, they took hold of his words and streamed to the wilderness to be baptized in preparation.

> WE GO TO THE DEPTH OF OUR INNERMOST BEING WHERE GOD'S PROMISED RIVERS OF LIVING WATER FLOW AND CRY OUT TO GOD LIKE NEVER BEFORE.

Unlike Ahaz, therefore, with whom the Lord was angry, we reach deep inside ourselves and pull up the passion. We go to the furnace of our soul where the pilot light has gone out and ignite it again. We go to the depth of our innermost being where God's promised rivers of living water flow and cry out to God like we never have before. We do it because it's right—and the alternative is death. We do it not as beggars, but as royalty. We do it not as supplicants before the throne, but as ministers of the Most High God who receive their orders from the King and who then proclaim and enforce the Lord's decrees in the land.

To lay hold of the request for a sign that God sought from Ahaz, we're going to have to latch on to the truth that our God can do *anything*, far beyond our understanding.

Now to Him who is able to do far more abundantly beyond all that we ask or think, according to the power that works within us, to Him be the glory in the church and in Christ Jesus to all generations forever and ever. Amen.

(Ephesians 3:20–21)

4

WHAT IS HAPPENING TO OUR NATION?

A great outpouring of the Spirit of God hovers over us, ready to descend in power and blessing, but we must prepare to receive it and be ready to minister to a world in need. What is happening to our nation and our world? If we expect to respond appropriately, we must understand how we have come to this point. This chapter ends in a word of hope and victory, a promise to believers, but first, I must paint a picture of the situation and explain how it has developed.

Obviously, violent confrontations have been seen and reported around the country. There have been riots in our streets. Vicious attempts at character assassination have been directed at good men by people who lie. Words of hatred and name-calling have been hurled back and forth. Each side claims righteousness and innocence while calling the other side evil. Racial divisions have deepened. The year 2018 saw eleven deaths in a synagogue shooting in Pittsburgh, just one of many incidents involving places of worship, schools, workplaces, and even entertainment venues. Families break up. Crime rates rise. Now add an opioid epidemic to our burgeoning drug problem. At this writing, a crisis at the U.S. southern border gains intensity while the U.S. Congress remains paralyzed by partisan bickering. Lawlessness increases.

Why?

IDOLATRY BRINGS HATRED

While our nation—and the culture of the world—has become bitterly divided by political conflict, the problem doesn't stem from political differences. Hatred finds its source in idolatry. As human beings, God made us for worship. We inevitably fall down and worship at some altar, no matter what it might be. We can't help ourselves. Because God created us this way, we are hardwired to devote ourselves either to God or something that stands in His place. We compulsively give our devotion to causes, goals, ideas, or even fellow human beings—anything or anyone offering a promise of transcendent power over life and circumstances. No culture has ever been without its object of worship, its idea of God.

> WE ARE HARDWIRED TO DEVOTE OURSELVES EITHER TO GOD OR SOMETHING THAT STANDS IN HIS PLACE.

Hindus in India have thousands of gods. Asians may revere Buddha. Arabs worship Allah. We believers in Jesus have Christianity, the religion, but not necessarily always a true relationship with Jesus. Even communist countries are never truly as atheistic as they claim to be because in reality, they deify the state, its philosophy, or its primary leader. North Korea's "dear leader" and "Shining Sun," Kim Jong-un, tolerates no dissent or devotion to any other god.

Trust me, anyone who claims to be an atheist has a faith. It might be faith in themselves or humanism, the exaltation of humanity and its supposed goodness. Intellect might become one's altar, or the supposed greatness of the human spirit. Nationalism can become a form of religion. When one's country, race, or ethnicity becomes a primary identity or source of power and transcendent purpose, even when informed by our Christian faith, it has become idolatry. At that point, hatred, abuse, and exploitation become inevitable. Your idol might be a pursuit of power and money to fill the inner vacuum, but it remains idolatry.

The point is that something will take the place of God and will attract your worship. It's inevitable. Whether you know it or not, you *will* have faith in something that you believe gives you power over life and a sense of importance or significance. Apart from devotion to the one true God, something that's *not* God will take up residence at the center of your life and you'll seek to draw strength from it as it promises to empower you or create a good feeling.

Where idolatry goes, hate will always follow, sometimes in obvious forms and sometimes in forms much less subtle. I don't believe there's an in-between, and we see the growing hatred now consuming nations and cultures. You can either walk with the God of love and be consumed by who and what He is, or you can be consumed by forms of hate flowing from some other source.

YOU CAN EITHER WALK WITH THE GOD OF LOVE OR BE CONSUMED BY FORMS OF HATE FLOWING FROM SOME OTHER SOURCE.

YOU SHALL HAVE NO OTHER GODS...

When giving Moses the Ten Commandments, God made it clear that He alone was to be worshiped:

> *I am the* LORD *your God, who brought you out of the land of Egypt, out of the house of slavery. You shall have no other gods before Me. You shall not make for yourself an idol, or any likeness of what is in heaven above or on the earth beneath or in the water under the earth. You shall not worship them or serve them; for I, the* LORD *your God, am a jealous God, visiting the iniquity of the fathers on the children, on the third and the fourth generations of those who hate Me, but showing lovingkindness to thousands, to those who love Me and keep My commandments.*
>
> (Exodus 20:2–6)

In other words, God was saying, "It was My power and love that delivered you from Egypt. You shall turn to no other power for life or deliverance. There can be no other source, no other god, no other name, and no other creator."

PUSHING GOD OUT

In light of all this, what happens when an individual begins to write God out of the picture? What consequences ensue when a culture pushes God to the side, or when it denies God altogether? What happens when a person or a nation forgets or turns away from what Jesus called *"the great and foremost commandment,"* which is *"You shall love the Lord your God with all your heart, and with all your soul, and with all your mind"* (Matthew 22:38, 37)?

The answer is that *we inevitably turn to other sources and make of them a sacred religion.* Our built-in hunger to worship something cannot be denied. It never dies. It's in our nature. We might not call it worship, but that's what it is, and we'll defend it with ferocious devotion. It will always be the easier path, the less demanding road, the way of least resistance, the path that asks less of us while it promises more, but robs us instead. If a nation, as a nation, rejects God, something will take God's place and whether or not you call it God, it will promise power over life and situations. Then because it is *not* God, it will unleash hatred when challenged.

> OUR NATION AND WORLD CULTURE HAVE REPLACED GOD WITH PHILOSOPHIES, ASSUMPTIONS, JUDGMENTS, AND POLITICAL STANCES. THE UNAVOIDABLE RESULT IS CONFLICT AND HATRED.

Our nation and world culture have replaced God with a long list of philosophies, assumptions, judgments, and political stances. The unavoidable result is conflict and hatred. God is love and truth. Everything else leads to hatred, deception, and lies. This choice of something other than the one true God as a source explains why Israel rejected the prophets and stoned or imprisoned them. Those prophets of old challenged the false gods that people had exalted to the place of the one true God and they incurred the people's wrath.

ATTACKING THE PROPHETS

They threw Jeremiah down a well. They imprisoned Micaiah and gave him meager rations of bread and water. They crucified Jesus, and later whipped and beat the apostle Paul, stoned him, and left him for dead. Every one of them confronted what people worshiped in place of the one true God, our Father. When you confront someone's false god, they take offense and react with violence and anger.

The goal of the prophets in ancient Israel was always to purify the hunger and desire of the people for something to worship, the built-in, undeniable tendency to worship a god. Speaking for God, the prophets sought to deliver the people from all that would falsely promise power, victory over circumstances, prosperity, and well-being. They called Israel to purity of devotion to the one God, but the people kept putting other gods in His place and those false gods made promises they could never keep. In the end, demonically fueled self-focus led them to sacrifice their children by fire to Molech. Sound familiar? Witness the current abortion holocaust!

After literally centuries of prophetic warnings, God sent the Babylonians to conquer Israel, destroy the temple and Jerusalem, and carry the cream of the population into exile. As God's last resort, this demonstration of His wrath permanently cured the nation of worshiping idols. Nevertheless, by the time of Jesus, they had substituted another god for the one true God and thought that what they put in His place *was* God. That idol was the Law—as interpreted and applied by the Pharisees in the form of rules that went well beyond what was actually included in the first five books of the Bible.

IDOLIZING THE LAW

Israel made a god out of God's Word and His Law. Confusing devotion to the Law with purified devotion to God, they began to worship the Law itself. When they did this, they began to misinterpret and misapply God's Law. The inevitable happened. Love was lost. God Himself is love, but love of the Law morphed into subtle forms of hatred—hatred for Gentiles, hatred for sinners who didn't live by the Pharisees' interpretation of the Law, and hatred for people who fell into immorality. With God, love flows. With idolatry, hatred grows under the guise of forms of love, although those captivated by this form of idolatry will call it love. Evil will be called good.

In Israel after the exile, legalism took root and with it came hatred for anyone who didn't walk according to the way of the Pharisees and see devotion to God as they did. Violence resulted, both to the soul and in the flesh. Prophets were stoned. Sinners were shunned. Jesus was crucified.

IDOLATRY TODAY

In modern times, as we have driven God from public life, schools, and courtrooms, our political ideologies have become our idols. This has led to political correctness, accusations of racism, and even gender confusion and division. I know of people who have divorced because one supported Hillary Clinton for president while the other supported Donald Trump.

For many in our contemporary culture, marijuana has become a religion. No one would call it that, but all I need to do to attract angry attacks and ridiculous arguments is go to a social media site and write something about the evils and dangers of cannabis. People react with anger when you challenge their use of marijuana in almost the same way Muslims respond when you say something negative about Muhammed. It's demonically fueled and it elicits a demonic response. Why? Because marijuana makes false promises of power over things like emotions or stress, just as any false god does. In truth, users have surrendered power in order to be captivated by another power. Demons love these things because they function as substitutes for God.

Whenever we turn to something other than the one true God to obtain power over life, demonic forces—opportunists looking for ways to access and destroy what God loves—invade, energize, and ruin lives. Inevitably, you will worship either the God of love, or a false god that destroys, but you *will* worship something.

> INEVITABLY, YOU WILL WORSHIP EITHER THE GOD OF LOVE, OR A FALSE GOD THAT DESTROYS, BUT YOU WILL WORSHIP SOMETHING.

THE SEDUCTION OF IDOLATRY

Ancient Israel saw the nations around them prospering and wanted to be like them, to have what they had. Consequently, they gradually began to allow elements of the worship of Baal into their lives, along with certain ungodly and unbiblical beliefs, and they allowed those influences to infiltrate the way they worshiped God in order to gain the power they believed their neighbors had. It resulted in violence and the sacrifice of their children to Baal/Molech on the altar of their desire for wealth and power over life. Instead of bringing prosperity and power, however, it resulted in exploitation of the poor and neglect of the elderly.

People will always have a god. If they reject the one true God, they'll choose another. In some cases, they'll think that what they believe about that god *is* the one true God. God, however, is *love*. When any nation or culture chooses some other god to worship, they inherit the opposite of love because no other god can ever *be* love. Hatred results. Brokenness ensues in relationships and families. Separations and divisions break up societies. Wars erupt and violence destroys. History is replete with examples.

WHAT IS HAPPENING TO OUR NATION?

As we have written God out of public life, rejected His laws and principles, and experienced a decline in church attendance, other gods have taken the place of the one true God. In biblical times, hatred grew as Israel turned away from God. Throughout history, whenever nations or peoples have turned from the one true God who is love, hatred has taken His place. Because Satan comes disguised as an angel of light, hatred often masquerades as something good.

Hatred flows through those on the left masquerading as justice fighters for the middle class and the downtrodden. Hatred erupts from the right in the form of nationalism and love of country. It will even develop as well-meaning religious people apply God's laws without the love meant to temper them and draw people to repentance and redemption. Within the Christian community, we make gods out of our doctrines until believers hurl hatred and accusations at other believers for holding different views of the same passages of Scripture. How many have made the Bible their God instead of the One who wrote the Bible and then attacked people who love the move of the Holy Spirit?

> **WE SUFFER THE EFFECTS OF IDOLATRY IN ALL ITS VARIOUS FORMS IN OUR GOVERNMENTS, IN FAMILIES, AND IN THE CHURCH.**

What is happening to our nation and our world? We suffer the effects of idolatry in all its various forms in our governments, in families, and in the church. God is love. Worship anything else—seek power for life, strength, position, or significance from any other source—and hatred and division inevitably result.

SIX INDICTMENTS BROUGHT BY GOD

Seeking to save Israel, God brought six indictments against them, all based on idolatry.

REJECTION OF GOD'S LAW

According to Amos 2:4, they rejected the law of the Lord and did not keep His statutes. Even in the church, we see increasing compromise of basic morality and integrity. Hyper-grace—one of the most popular teachings in the body of Christ today—excuses that rejection of basic moral principles. The book of Proverbs sharpens the issue and describes what I see happening today: "*Those who forsake the law praise the wicked, but those who keep the law strive with them*" (Proverbs 28:4).

BELIEF IN LIES

Amos 2:4 continues: "*Their lies also have led them astray, those after which their fathers walked.*" In our culture, these lies involve both false gods and demonic philosophies and theologies. We now have postmodernism, cheap grace, the idea that repentance is a once-and-done deal if you're a Christian, denial of the existence of hell, universal salvation, and more.

ECONOMIC SELF-FOCUS

Amos 2:6 reads, "*They sell the righteous for money and the needy for a pair of sandals.*" In the western world, we worship at the altar of prosperity, captivated by a preoccupation with self. The name of this religion is Baalism, Canaan's fertility cult of prosperity that seduced Israel again and again and infiltrated the worship of the One God.

SEXUAL IMMORALITY

Of this, Amos 2:7 says, "*A man and his father resort to the same girl in order to profane My holy name.*" A study of Scripture reveals this verse is just one example of the types of sexual perversion and immorality that had become accepted in Israel. In our culture, sexual perversion and fornication have now come to be regarded as normal.

ARROGANCE

"These who pant after the very dust of the earth on the head of the helpless also turn aside the way of the humble" (Amos 2:7). In reality, neglect of obedience to God's laws and principles constitutes human arrogance against God because we position ourselves among those who believe they know more than He does about what makes life work.

Our culture actually mocks those who humbly submit to God's law, calling them backward, bigoted, divisive, or judgmental. Seldom are they honored who stand for God's moral standard. All of this tells us that false gods, masquerading as angels of light, have garnered the attention of the culture of our nation. Hatred results. Division results. Violence results.

POLLUTED AND COMPROMISED DEVOTION TO GOD

"But you made the Nazirites drink wine, and you commanded the prophets saying, 'You shall not prophesy!'" (Amos 2:12). In case you hadn't noticed, holiness preachers and prophets aren't too popular today! In Israel's case, God could not bless what did not reflect His own nature. The same will be true for us.

PENALTIES FOR IDOLATRY

MILITARY DEFEAT

When the enemy came against them, Israel would no longer enjoy the Lord's support for victory in battle, despite being well-equipped and strong. *"He who grasps the bow will not stand his ground, the swift of foot will not escape, nor will he who rides the horse save his life. Even the bravest among the warriors will flee naked in that day"* (Amos 2:15–16). When invading armies finally attacked, Israel crumbled.

Without a turning, it won't make any real difference how powerful our military becomes. We will be vulnerable. In recent years, America has enjoyed an extended period of grace that affects the entire world. We must treat this as a time for the church to get right with God, take up our destiny and walk as we have been called to walk to affect a nation and the world. Glory is coming in the midst of gathering darkness, a fresh anointing to shine in the midst, but our time to prepare is limited and the hour is urgent.

ECONOMIC COLLAPSE

The unprecedented prosperity that grew as a result of the Lord's favor upon Israel was revoked. Without a turning to the one true God, so it will be with the United States and the nations of the world. *"I will also smite the winter house together with the summer house"* (Amos 3:15). Because of U.S. world dominance economically, when we fall, we will take the rest of the world down with us. Our time to prepare for what's to come is limited. We must use the time allotted us as believers to build up our strength, our devotion, and our purity of focus on Jesus.

CLOSURE OF PLACES OF WORSHIP

"I will also punish the altars of Bethel; the horns of the altar will be cut off and they will fall to the ground" (Amos 3:14). Ultimately, God will not permit churches to continue in which His laws, His standards, His morality, His Word, and His nature of incomprehensible love are not honored, taught, and lived out. A reckoning will come.

It has already begun.

THE SPIRIT OF GOD IS MOVING

Here is our glory. Here in this hour, this strategic moment in history, we find our calling and destiny, our privilege and our honor. Among a growing, devoted remnant, the Spirit of God is bringing about a purity of focus on Jesus and the heart of the Father. I see it everywhere I travel. Characterized by a beautiful simplicity, the remnant exhibit no selfish ambition. It's not about recognition for the sake of building anyone's great kingdom, or seeking glory for anyone's name, or following after and idolizing some big name.

> AMONG A GROWING, DEVOTED REMNANT,
> THE SPIRIT OF GOD IS BRINGING ABOUT A PURITY OF FOCUS ON
> JESUS AND THE HEART OF THE FATHER.

Instead, it's about Jesus and Jesus alone, drinking of Him, knowing Him, and becoming sons and daughters who radiate His presence, love, and holiness wherever we go. Whenever we're around, people must be able to sense the love and healing, even at a distance. It's about nothing being more important to us than being with Jesus, no matter what the circumstances around us might be like. It's a place where joy and victory cannot be stolen, where trust and rest in Him cannot be threatened, shaken, or taken.

Whether natural born or grafted in, we who know Jesus are sons and daughters of Abraham, inheritors of the promise made to him concerning the calling on his life and progeny:

Indeed I will greatly bless you, and I will greatly multiply your seed as the stars of the heavens and as the sand which is on the seashore; and your seed shall possess the gate of their enemies. In your seed all the nations of the earth shall be blessed, because you have obeyed My voice.

(Genesis 22:17–18)

This is our inheritance, our role in the earth, that through us, the nations would be blessed with the Father's love and the revelation of who He is. We must not allow ourselves to become participants in the divisions and hatreds that flow from the idolatries surrounding us.

SERVING AS LEAVEN

Jesus taught us:

"The kingdom of heaven is like a mustard seed, which a man took and sowed in his field; and this is smaller than all other seeds, but when it is full grown, it is larger than the garden plants and becomes a tree, so that the birds of the air come and nest in its branches." He spoke another parable to them, "The kingdom of heaven is like leaven, which a woman took and hid in three pecks of flour until it was all leavened." (Matthew 13:31–33)

Leaven is the small bit of living organism, such as yeast, that's inserted into a large quantity of flour until it permeates the whole. It infiltrates and expands, changing the nature of the dough. Bread made with real yeast even tastes better and is more nutritious than bread made with other ingredients such as baking powder. We must be change agents in this world, not participants in its sickness. Our Father calls us to infiltrate the culture around us, to exert godly influence, because that's what leaven does. Where we go, the world changes just because we were there. Jesus never called us to withdraw. He called and anointed us to be fearless and undefeated world-changers. We win because our God is a God of victory. The world changes for the better where we walk because our God is the Creator and we're His kids who inherit from Him.

We are the firewall standing against destruction, the levee against the tsunami wave of hatred I have long prophesied that now engulfs us. I will never forget the Sunshine Mine fire back in 1971, when our family lived in Wallace, Idaho, where my father pastored. While I was away at college in 1972, ninety-one miners died of carbon monoxide poisoning. As rescue efforts were under way and the outcome remained uncertain, a crowd gathered at the entrance to the mine, threatening violence against the management. In the authority of the Lord, my father stepped between the two sides; with the authority of the Holy Spirit emanating through him, he defused the violence that was about to erupt. That kind of incident describes our role in this world, standing in peace against the mob to disarm their violence and hatred.

What is happening to our nation and our world right now is what happens whenever idolatry in any form takes root. It releases hatred in the name of love or the struggle for justice. If the enemy of our soul couldn't deceive people to think that evil is good, people would never fall for his deceptions. Those deceptions constitute a leaven that infiltrates and increases unless God's people rise to stop it by being a better and more powerful leaven. We are the firewall against the wave of hatred and idolatry tearing the nation and the world apart. We are the levee against the flood.

WE NEED TO TAKE RESPONSIBILITY

The general atmosphere of hatred loosed by idolatry has opened the way for multiple murders in schools and workplaces. Can we really blame perpetrators like this as if we're not part of it? Can the rest of us truly claim innocence? To what degree have we participated in the influence of the leaven of hatred inspired by cultural idolatry? All of us in this culture share responsibility for love grown cold, no matter what side of the political, moral or religious divide we stand on. Hatred and anger never ever bear good fruit, no matter what the provocation.

> ALL OF US IN THIS CULTURE SHARE RESPONSIBILITY FOR LOVE GROWN COLD, NO MATTER WHAT SIDE OF THE POLITICAL, MORAL OR RELIGIOUS DIVIDE WE STAND ON.

Never think that hatred for one thing or one group can exist in isolation, as if it applies only to politics, the cultural war, or only to the man who shoots up a school or a church or drives a conservative politician out of a restaurant. If you draw down the level of love in one area of life, you draw it down in *every other area of life* in the same way that cancer in one organ will metastasize into every other part of the body if not treated. Just a minuscule amount of hatred for one person or thing—just a vile word or two in another's ear—will affect families, churches, communities, and more. National repentance, with no one on any side claiming innocence, is the only remedy. Let it start with the body of Christ.

Then let us fulfill the destiny for which the Holy Spirit has filled us.

> *You are the light of the world. A city set on a hill cannot be hidden; nor does anyone light a lamp and put it under a basket, but on the lampstand, and it gives light to all who are in the house. Let your light shine before men in such a way that they may see your good works, and glorify your Father who is in heaven.*   (Mathew 5:14–16)

Let Romans 8:19 be manifested in us, *"For the anxious longing of the creation waits eagerly for the revealing of the sons of God,"* as we radiate the presence of the living God in purity and holiness to redeem a world in the Father's love.

5

WHAT MUST WE DO?

What can we, as dedicated, sold-out believers, do in this critical period of history? What is God asking of us? What is the first step?

THE CALL TO REPENTANCE

Since the time of the Babylonian exile, people have turned to 2 Chronicles for answers.

> *If I shut up the heavens so that there is no rain, or if I command the locust to devour the land, or if I send pestilence among My people, and My people who are called by My name humble themselves and pray and seek My face and turn from their wicked ways, then I will hear from heaven, will forgive their sin and will heal their land.*
> (2 Chronicles 7:13–14)

And so we pray. But I often wonder if we stop reading where it says to pray and seek the Lord, but fail to move to the next line, *"turn from their wicked ways."* Prayer that changes a nation begins with repentance.

In a culture steeped in unbiblical ideas of individualism, you might ask, "What do I have to repent of? I don't commit fornication or adultery. I don't do drugs. I don't lie, steal, or cheat. I serve others to the best of my ability. What's left?" Scripture, however, thinks in corporate terms, God's people as a collective unit. *"My people who are called by My name"* indicates a plurality, a group of people addressed as if they were one entity, one person. Bible scholars call this the *principle of solidarity*. Biblically speaking, we exist as one entity, inextricably connected with one another without sacrificing our essential individuality. More than this, we stand in solidarity with the generations who've gone before us, as if we were all one person. For instance, Israel, in all its millions, is collectively named Jacob after the patriarch from whom they trace their ancestry.

> WE MUST CRY OUT IN REPENTANCE NOT JUST FOR OURSELVES AS INDIVIDUALS, BUT ALSO FOR OUR NATION, OUR CULTURE, AND OUR CHURCH.

If the people of God, called by His name, choose to humble themselves, pray, and turn away from their wicked ways, then God will forgive and restore their broken land. Here lies a pivotal principle. It might be better for us to stop crying out for God to do something like revival and begin to cry out in repentance for ourselves as individuals, our nation as a whole, our culture in which we participate, and our church as the body of Christ. We must do this as a people together *so that* God can do something like revival.

NEHEMIAH'S PRAYER: IDENTIFICATIONAL REPENTANCE

And so we come to Nehemiah. After literally decades stretching into centuries, during which Israel refused to listen to the warnings of the prophets to turn away from idolatry and went so far as to sacrifice their children to Baal/Molech, God finally had to act. In 586 BC, the Babylonian army conquered Judah and utterly destroyed Jerusalem. The people spent seventy years of exile in Babylon.

As those years drew to a close, messengers came from Jerusalem with a report they delivered to Nehemiah in Babylon concerning conditions in Judah and Jerusalem among those who remained in the land. *"They said to me, 'The remnant there in the province who survived the captivity are in great distress and reproach, and the wall of Jerusalem is broken down and its gates are burned with fire'"* (Nehemiah 1:3).

The news broke Nehemiah's heart and he spent days weeping and mourning over what he'd heard. But then he prayed. Nehemiah held a high-ranking official position as cupbearer to the king. Anyone attempting to assassinate Artaxerxes by means of poison had to get past Nehemiah. In that position of trust, Nehemiah had become highly skilled in administration. He knew well how to organize people and get things done. Love for his homeland birthed a desperate longing to go to Jerusalem, serve as governor of the province, and restore the walls of the city for his people and homeland. This, however, required release and favor from the king. Only God could make that happen, and so Nehemiah turned to prayer: *"I beseech You, O Lord God of heaven, the great and awesome God, who preserves the covenant and lovingkindness for those who love Him and keep His commandments"* (Nehemiah 1:5). He began with praise and an affirmation of who God really is. The most effective prayer begins with hope, confessions, and declarations regarding the nature of God. You don't have to actually feel it, but as you do it, you channel your heart and spirit in a positive direction.

Nehemiah prayed:

> *Let Your ear now be attentive and Your eyes open to hear the prayer of Your servant which I am praying before You now, day and night, on behalf of the sons of Israel Your servants, confessing the sins of the sons of Israel which we have sinned against You; I and my father's house have sinned. We have acted very corruptly against You and have not kept the commandments, nor the statutes, nor the ordinances which You commanded Your servant Moses.*
>
> (Nehemiah 1:6–7)

Nehemiah understood that the destruction of his homeland and the exile to Babylon were the direct results of turning away from the Lord and compromising His commandments. Although he himself was a righteous man, he confessed sin and repented for it *in solidarity* with his people as if all their sins, as well as his forebears', were his own. Rather than stand above and apart from them, he identified with them and owned the collective sin of Israel personally. We call this *identificational repentance.*

Nehemiah continued:

> *Remember the word which You commanded Your servant Moses, saying, "If you are unfaithful I will scatter you among the peoples; but if you return to Me and keep My commandments and do them, though those of you who have been scattered were in the most remote part of the heavens, I will gather them from there and will bring them to the place where I have chosen to cause My name to dwell." They are Your servants and Your people whom You redeemed by*

Your great power and by Your strong hand.
(Nehemiah 1:8–10)

Having laid the groundwork in repentance, Nehemiah peititioned the Lord to act—not first by asking God to do something to change the situation, but by repenting for the sin of his people *so that* God could act on their behalf.

Arguments about grace would be useless at this point. God always loves. Even in their idolatry and sin, Israel never ceased to be God's people whom He loved. Nehemiah affirmed this in his prayer. You and I never cease to be His, no matter how far we wander. However, regardless of how much He loves us, God can never bless sin. He is holy. His nature will not allow Him to pour out blessing on unrighteousness.

> REGARDLESS OF HOW MUCH HE LOVES US, GOD CAN NEVER BLESS SIN. HIS NATURE WILL NOT ALLOW HIM TO POUR OUT BLESSING ON UNRIGHTEOUSNESS.

Nehemiah therefore prayed:

O Lord, I beseech You, may Your ear be attentive to the prayer of Your servant and the prayer of Your servants who delight to revere Your name, and make Your servant successful today and grant him compassion before this man.
(Nehemiah 1:11)

The result was that the king not only released Nehemiah to go, but paid for the trip, gave him an armed guard, and authorized materials to rebuild the wall and restore the city. All of this took place in response to identificational confession and repentance. God sent favor and moved the heart of a pagan king.

Do we want to change our nation and our world? Do we want a move of God to rock the church and the culture around us? Then heed the lesson from Nehemiah.

IDENTIFICATIONAL REPENTANCE IN THE NEW TESTAMENT

One might ask, is this corporate repentance thing in the New Testament? Is the need for ongoing repentance even part of the new covenant? In the book of Revelation, for example, the angel called for corporate, collective repentance on the part of the church in Ephesus:

> *Therefore remember from where you have fallen, and repent and do the deeds you did at first; or else I am coming to you and will remove your lampstand out of its place—unless you repent.*   (Revelation 2:5)

For falling into the teaching of the Nicolaitans (first century hyper-grace, cheap grace), God warned the church in Permamum (see Revelation 2:12) to repent in solidarity as a people. I'm certain there were people in Pergamum who hadn't bought into false teaching, but the angel addressed it as a corporate guilt. The whole body stood defiled by it, the innocent with the guilty. We're connected. The sin of my brothers and sisters affects me as well.

> *"To the angel of the church in Sardis write: He who has the seven Spirits of God and the seven stars, says this: 'I know your deeds, that you have a name that you are alive, but you are dead. Wake up, and strengthen the things that remain, which were about to die; for I have not found your deeds completed in the sight of My God. So remember what you have received and heard; and keep it, and repent.'"*
>   (Revelation 3:1–3)

Again, I have no doubt that there were people in Sardis on fire for the Lord, not personally guilty of the Lord's indictment. As a whole, however, they had lost their fire. God called for them to repent as a church, as a single connected entity.

> IF YOU'VE BEEN LISTENING TO THOSE WHO SAY THAT ONCE YOU'VE GIVEN YOUR LIFE TO JESUS, YOU NEVER NEED TO REPENT AGAIN, YOU'RE BEING SEDUCED BY A DESTRUCTIVE LIE.

Clearly, if you've been listening to those who say that once you've given your life to Jesus, you never need to repent again, you are hearing cheap grace, not real grace. You're being seduced by a destructive lie. Those who perpetrate this lie lead God's people astray and hold back the full blessing of God. One day they will stand before His throne and be held accountable for defiling the Lord's bride.

WHAT ABOUT AMERICA AND WESTERN CULTURE?

Are we corporately guilty in America and western culture? Are we guilty of sin as a people? Do you and I share responsibility for the moral and ethical corruption that has engulfed us, and the violence it releases? Before you answer, pull away from looking only at yourself; consider what I'm saying, and take a lesson from Nehemiah.

Do we want to change the church? Do we long to see a nation redeemed? Condemnation, judgment, and angry cries will never accomplish that purpose. Never can we realize the purposes of God by standing apart and protesting our own righteousness against the sin and defilement of the culture in which we live. Blasting the liberal left as demonic, or the conservative right as immoral, won't do it. That kind of thing only perpetuates division and shuts off favor from both man and God.

Are any of us innocent of the sin of our people collectively? The answer is no. Let me suggest something: if there is racism in America, for instance, and if you are an American citizen, no matter what race your genes tell you that you are, it won't play well before the throne of heaven for me or you to protest our individual innocence. Each of us, individually, exists as part of a people, a collective entity that bears the guilt as one. We're part of a system, demonically inspired, and caught up in a web woven by the enemy of our soul to entrap and destroy people of every ethnic or racial group and, most especially, the church, the Lord's bride. If immorality runs rampant in the nation, it won't do to protest that I am individually innocent of fornication, adultery, perversion, or addiction. I'm part of a nation, a people, a collective entity, a connected culture that makes all this possible.

> **WE'RE PART OF A SYSTEM, DEMONICALLY INSPIRED, AND CAUGHT UP IN A WEB WOVEN BY THE ENEMY OF OUR SOUL TO ENTRAP AND DESTROY PEOPLE.**

You might ask, "How can this be?" As lovers of superhero films and stories, my wife and I went to see *Aquaman* at the nearest multiplex theater. Good movie! No problem! No sex! No cursing! But Warner Bros. Pictures, the company that produced *Aquaman*, also produces films that promote immorality and unrighteousness, such as *Joker*, *IT*, and *Birds of Prey*. Our ticket purchase helped to fund those other films that condition the culture around us to accept immorality as normal and even righteous. In this culture, I can't escape this kind of aiding and abetting without becoming a monk in isolation, disconnected from the society around me, and therefore unable to effectively speak into it to reach people. But my ticket purchase funded a company that conditions a culture to accept sin as normal and good. It's the collective sin of my people and I'm part of it, whether I choose to be or not.

At home, regardless of what I might choose to watch on television, my cable bill likewise pays for the conditioning of my culture to accept vileness as normal. That same culture then calls me a bigot if I don't agree with its claims. My purchases at stores fund donations the unrighteous make to causes opposed to the gospel of Jesus. At election time, we collectively put ungodly people in public office.

You and I pay for abortions, whether we want to or not, because our taxes support abortuaries through agencies funded by tax dollars. The U.S. Congress maintains a slush fund at our expense to pay off people who accuse congressmen of sexual misconduct. Unless we want to refuse to pay our taxes and find ourselves under prosecution, we participate in the mess and share the guilt. We can't avoid it. As part of this collective identity, we can and must pray as Nehemiah prayed in identificational repentance.

> WE CAN AND MUST PRAY AS NEHEMIAH PRAYED IN IDENTIFICATIONAL REPENTANCE.

A PRAYER FOR THE NATION

Lord, grant this nation more time, Your people more time. Intervene in D.C. Convict the heart of our president. Convict the hateful Democrats and Republicans who are at each others' throats. Let Your Spirit prevail once more. We have sinned and violated Your precepts. We have failed in the promise You gave this nation. We have not spoken in terms of grace. We have been quick to speak and quick to anger. We have approved of what is not right. Even Your people have wandered away in compromise. Have mercy. Forgive us, Lord. We have lost our way. You have warned and we have not heard. You have called us and we have not listened. Your mercies are new every morning. Come, pour out Your blessing yet this once more. Hold us in Your arms this once more. And let Your people, Your remnant, shine like the sun in a dark time!

I prayed that prayer on Christmas Eve 2018. A day or so later, in response to a question someone asked me, the Lord spoke. In the form of my own musings, I wrote down my impression of what He said. Here it is, copied directly from my prayer journal:

MUSINGS ON THE LORD'S MESSAGE

Over the years, I've warned of the influence of the spirit of Baal and how that demonic thing influences the mass mentality. Israel struggled with it and we struggle in the same way. All four biblical marks of that influence are dominant in our culture…self-focus, immorality, murder of the innocents, and cutting. We're saturated with it through media and the people around us every day and it deafens us as a culture to the call of God and the heart of the gospel, what it means to be disciples. As a result we define "growth" as personal prosperity, personal happiness, and personal, individual benefit.

God, however, defines it in terms of growth in relationship, growth in covenant with Him and with one another. Do we work it out together? Forgive? Talk things through? Repent when we fail in relationship or in some other way? Do we seek God's heart for the sake of relationship with Him and others?

The heart of Paul's letters turns on just two issues— the doctrine of salvation by grace through faith, and relationships that reflect the oneness of Father, Son, and Holy Spirit. Baal attacks all of that. Most Christians are exposed to just an hour or two of church per week and *maybe* the message there is truly reflective of God's kingdom culture.

The rest of the week, we're bombarded by the spirit of the culture. And we too often resist spending the time outside of Sunday services to attend a cell group or a class or a prayer meeting where relationships and cove- nant can grow.

WE NEED TO BE WILLING TO REPENT

Long ago, Isaiah prophesied, *"For thus the Lord GOD, the Holy One of Israel, has said, 'In repentance and rest you will be saved, in quietness and trust is your strength'"* (Isaiah 30:15). The last half of the verse says Israel was unwilling to repent and trust God for His ways. In the end, it cost them their nation.

Let us be a willing people. Can we weep like Nehemiah over the condition of our nation, the body of Christ, and our local churches? Every truly great revival that has swept the United States, or any other nation, began in repentance and in tra- vailing prayer with a focus on the blood of Jesus that cleanses us from sin. Then, on the heels of repentance, came joy, free- dom, miracles, and healing of individuals, families, and society. The glory that fell invited and compelled others to repent and become part of it.

THE ENEMY OF OUR SOUL IS AFRAID OF A REPENTANT PEOPLE WHO UNDERSTAND WHAT NEHEMIAH UNDERSTOOD.

What the enemy of our soul fears most is not the miracles, our revival meetings, or our packed-out churches. He's not afraid of people praying the sinner's prayer at the altar. He's afraid of a repentant people who understand what Nehemiah understood. These are the people who together as one will rebuild ruined cities and restore strength to the people of God. These are the people who, in their oneness, will influence kings and rulers to turn the tide of history.

Upon returning to the land, Nehemiah organized the people to rebuild the walls of the city. He did it in the face of vicious opposition from much of the surrounding population and was successful in it because he had the Lord's favor. It all began with his prayer of identificational repentance for both his own sins and the sins of his people that went back generations.

THE FRUIT OF REPENTANCE

When the people finished rebuilding the wall, Ezra the priest brought the scrolls of the law before the gathered people and began to read. This led to Nehemiah 9:1–3:

> *Now on the twenty-fourth day of this month the sons of Israel assembled with fasting, in sackcloth and with dirt upon them. The descendants of Israel separated themselves from all foreigners, and stood and confessed their sins and the iniquities of their fathers. While they stood in their place, they read from the book of the law of the LORD their God for a fourth of the day; and for another fourth they confessed and worshiped the LORD their God.*

With travail and weeping, the people repented and then worshiped and blessed God as they found themselves caught up in the wonder of all that God had done for them. They remembered and rejoiced in the Lord who had not only enabled their return from exile and the rebuilding of the walls, but who had brought them out of Egypt at the beginning, performed miracles of deliverance and provision, and gave them the Promised Land. Then, as if to seal their joy with a final cleansing, they finished once more with confession of how they had failed the Lord.

SPIRIT-INSPIRED CONVICTION

Just prior to the crucifixion, Jesus said:

But I tell you the truth, it is to your advantage that I go away; for if I do not go away, the Helper will not come to you; but if I go, I will send Him to you. And He, when He comes, will convict the world concerning sin and righteousness and judgment. (John 16:7–8)

When the Holy Spirit comes, He exposes sin and brings conviction. He does this for our sake and for our freedom. When I see His perfection, I see my own imperfection and the imperfection of my people with whom I stand in solidarity.

Freedom comes because in confession, I admit my own failings and my own participation in the collective sin of my people. I can then lift it up to God as He takes it from me. Every successfully recovering addict knows what I'm saying. This is step five of the Twelve Steps of Recovery: "I admitted to God, to myself, and to another human being the exact nature of my wrongs." In making that confession, repentance comes and freedom is released.

IDENTIFICATIONAL REPENTANCE REMOVES SELF-RIGHTEOUS CONDEMNATION AND THE HARSH RHETORIC THAT ERECT A BARRIER BETWEEN US AND THE WORLD.

The same dynamic applies to the kind of identificational repentance Nehemiah offered. It removes self-righteous condemnation and the harsh rhetoric that erect a barrier between us and the world, which prevent them from seeing Jesus in us and serve to discredit us in the eyes of those we wish to win. Identificational repentance says to God, "I'm not pleading my own innocence or exalting myself in self-righteousness." It removes the pointing of the finger, the accusing and the judging, and it says to our culture, "I'm with you. I'm here for you." It changes the tone of every interaction with people in life. Ultimately, it moves the hearts of kings, rulers, employers, and neighbors. It releases favor.

As disciples of Jesus, we are called as a people to change nations and workplaces, to affect cultures and alter the spiritual climate, as well as the natural one. We are called to influence kings and rulers, senators and congressmen.

IDENTIFICATIONAL REPENTANCE ON THREE LEVELS

First, what is my personal sin? Where have I contributed in any way to division in the body of Christ? What are my compromises in morality or character? Where have I judged, condemned, or fed disunity? By anyone's estimation, the church in this world remains a divided people, full of criticism, judgment, and condemnation.

I personally know that I must repent for any way in which I myself have contributed to this defilement out of my own brokenness, and I repent on behalf of the people of God for all the ways in which we together have harmed or dishonored the name of the Lord and alienated those He died to save. I pray, "Lord, we have judged, we have been critical, we have justified separation and division. Have mercy and restore us."

Second, we must engage in repentance for sins of the wider body of Christ. I pray, "Lord, we have been an unfaithful people. We have compromised morality and blessed abomination. We've been lukewarm. We have prophesied falsely and discredited Your name. We have judged and condemned where You offered grace. We have spoken in anger when we knew that anger does not accomplish Your righteousness. We have hidden ourselves and not reached out to sinners around us. Have mercy and forgive. Restore us as You always have in Your love that never fails."

Third, as one with the nation, we must repent for our national sins—our hatred, our division, our approval of immorality, our open rejection of God, our condemnations issued in the name of false righteousness, and our lawlessness as a people.

How do you change a nation? It begins with God's people in identificational repentance. Just as did Nehemiah, we confess that *we* have sinned. We cry, "Forgive us!"

It all comes down to that one line in Nehemiah's prayer, "*Confessing the sins of the sons of Israel which we have sinned against You; I and my father's house have sinned. We have acted very corruptly against You*" (Nehemiah 1:6–7). He reminds God of His promise to Moses: "*Though those of you who have been scattered were in the most remote part of the heavens, I will gather them from there and will bring them to the place where I have chosen to cause My name to dwell*" (Nehemiah 1:9).

REPENTANCE: THE CALL OF THE HOUR

The word of the hour is holiness. Unholiness will not stand in the crises soon to come upon this world. We have a limited time in which to prepare for these things. We've been appointed for victory, but no athlete who expects to win the game begins running laps the day before the big day. He or she does this in the months leading up to it. A promise has been made to us, but it won't happen automatically. It comes to pass only if we're prepared to receive it.

> *Arise, shine; for your light has come, and the glory of the* LORD *has risen upon you. For behold, darkness will cover the earth and deep darkness the peoples; but the* LORD *will rise upon you and His glory will appear upon you. Nations will come to your light, and kings to the brightness of your rising.*   (Isaiah 60:1–3)

Fulfillment of Isaiah's prophecy now lies before us. We must not be lulled to sleep. We cannot continue in old ways. Prayer is vital, but it must include humbling ourselves as a people to turn together from wicked ways. Because God is holy, He cannot and will not bless what is not holy. Right now, a great tug of war is being waged in this nation and in the church of Jesus Christ between the holy and the unholy, between right and wrong, between clean and unclean. We face an hour of decision that will determine our future for decades to come.

I repent personally, therefore, for all the good things that I have not been or done for all these years of my life. I choose to do more damage to the kingdom of darkness and walk in more joy and more victory in the last quarter of my life than in all my previous years combined. Let us together become nation-changers, whatever nation or culture we hail from. Let it begin with confession and repentance, both personal and identificatory, now and going forward.

6

WHAT DO I SEE?

PRELIMINARIES, REVIEW AND QUALIFIERS

The kind of identificational repentance I wrote of in the last chapter brings change to nations and cultures, but that's not actually its first purpose. If repenting on behalf of the church, our nation, or our culture begins with a goal of bringing change around us, we're probably headed in the wrong direction. Second Chronicles 7:14 reads, *"And My people who are called by My name humble themselves and pray and seek My face and turn from their wicked ways, then I will hear from heaven, will forgive their sin and will heal their land."* The key words are "humble themselves."

If our starting point is to cause change in the culture around us, and if we're measuring the effectiveness of our prayers of repentance by what we see changing in the world, then it's likely we'll not take the conviction deeply enough into our own hearts. In reality, we'll be unwittingly exalting ourselves above others in whom we want to see change, and we won't meet the requirement to humble ourselves. Failing that requirement, we won't see change in ourselves individually or as a body of Christ, and if we don't see change in ourselves, then the world won't be affected by us. Our impact on the culture around us will be muted. This can only lead to disappointment and discouragement.

When we repent on behalf of our nation, change will certainly happen, but it will come through our own pursuit of humility and our identification with the sins of our people, not from exalting ourselves over them, condemning their perceived unrighteousness, and positioning ourselves as the righteous ones. If we don't humbly radiate the Father's heart in the power of the Holy Spirit in a clean and pure way, we will garner little favor either from God or the world. Nehemiah received favor from Artaxerxes after his prayer of identificational repentance because he humbled himself personally as well as on behalf his people.

Daniel drew favor from Nebuchadnezzar by serving him; he humbled himself. Joseph drew favor and ascended to a high position in Egypt by using his prophetic gift to serve Pharaoh. Humility again. So, the first thing to keep in mind with identificational repentance is that it changes *us* before it changes the world around us.

> IDENTIFICATIONAL REPENTANCE CHANGES US BEFORE IT CHANGES THE WORLD AROUND US.

If I'm repenting on behalf of the body of Christ as well as for my nation or culture in its division, hatred, and immorality, identifying with the people of whom I am a part, and if I am taking responsibility for participation in it, then I'm much more likely to be transformed into a source of grace and love that can then affect change in others. Repentance on behalf of the church, my nation, and my culture will bring change, but I must not do it with a primary goal of bringing change. I must do it first for the sake of cleansing, holiness, and change in myself. I want to see differently. I want to respond differently. I want to be different in my own heart. I want to be a Holy Spirit-empowered magnet for the lost and the broken. In humility of this kind, power is perfected.

We can take a major step away from being self-righteous, judgmental, religious fools who unwittingly get caught up in the hateful spirit of the world by repenting in identification with the world we're part of. This changes our perspective and replaces anger with holy grief. It replaces judgment with life-changing grace, hatred with love, and despair with hope.

This brings me to the predictive portions of this prophetic word.

THE CHURCH

Anyone teaching or prophesying that God is somehow done with the organized church has it all wrong. The church has always been and will always be at the center of the Lord's plan for His people. No matter how ugly or off-base she may be, she remains His bride. According to 1 Corinthians 12, we are baptized by the Holy Spirit into the body of Christ. The Holy Spirit is the baptizer while the medium into which we are immersed is the body of Christ, the church. In the days to come, Jesus will be working with His church to purify and prepare us for what must come upon the world, our role in glory, and ultimately for His own return. We must allow ourselves to be immersed in fellowship.

> THE CHURCH WILL ALWAYS BE AT THE CENTER OF THE LORD'S PLAN
> FOR HIS PEOPLE. NO MATTER HOW UGLY OR OFF-BASE SHE MAY BE,
> SHE REMAINS HIS BRIDE.

EXPOSURE OF UNRIGHTEOUSNESS AND BROKENNESS

In January 2019, the Lord spoke this to me in prayer: "Many leaders will fall who have not let Me instruct them. They will fall by My hand. I will not allow My sheep to be led astray. I will place them in the hands of shepherds who will lead them in My ways."

He followed up with Ezekiel 34:2, *"Woe, shepherds of Israel who have been feeding themselves! Should not the shepherds feed the flock?"*

We now enter a period of time like the one Jesus spoke of in Luke 12:2–3:

> *But there is nothing covered up that will not be revealed, and hidden that will not be known. Accordingly, whatever you have said in the dark will be heard in the light, and what you have whispered in the inner rooms will be proclaimed upon the housetops.*

As early as the 1980s, God began exposing and cleansing sin in high places of Christian leadership, and the exposures have not stopped. In the days to come, such exposures will accelerate as God cleanses and prepares us for trials in the world and for His end time outpouring of the Holy Spirit. It won't just apply to leadership. Because of what is about to come upon the world, and because of what God is about to pour out, holiness matters more deeply for all of God's people.

The psalmist wrote, *"Righteousness and justice are the foundation of His throne"* (Psalm 97:2). If God does not deal with sin and brokenness in us individually, as a people, and in leadership, then the very foundations of the universe crumble. He cannot therefore allow His name to be dishonored without risking greater destruction for everyone. In His love, therefore, He *must* act. He may delay exposure and judgment for a season in order to give time for conviction and repentance. He'll send warnings and invitations, but there comes a time when He must act. We have reached that point. Now.

In fact, God is saying, "Start now to seek Me to expose your sin and brokenness. Confess and repent while trespasses remain small and easily addressed or I will expose them when sin is full grown and not so easily remedied." This applies to everyone. We're together in this, but it applies especially to leaders who stand under a greater accountability before the throne of heaven for the people whose lives they affect.

This is not because God is harsh or unforgiving. Quite the opposite! He loves us and needs us whole and clean for our own sake, for the sake of His name, and for the sake of the kingdom of God. Exposure of sin expresses His love because, ultimately, if we in leadership, or you in your home, continue in brokenness and sin, then God must move in some form of judgment to protect others from the damage our sin creates.

HERETICAL DOCTRINES AND COMPROMISES

The faithful know that in recent years, we have seen heretical doctrines proliferate in the church. Universalism. Open theism. Gay marriage. Acceptance of sexual activity outside the bonds of marriage. Denial of the need for repentance once saved. Hyper-grace. We've seen a growing trend to tamp down the importance of worship until in many places, there remains little or no room, or time, for God to freely move. Too often, it seems we feed the cult of the contemporary worship superstar rather than release the power of the body of Christ fully engaged as a people.

> A HUNGRY REMNANT GROWS IN PASSION AND STRENGTH.
> THEY CRAVE THE GENUINE; THEY'RE TIRED OF HYPE
> AND WEARY OF THE SHOW.

A hungry remnant, however, now grows in passion and strength. They long for the fullness. They crave the genuine and will not stand for anything less. They're tired of hype and weary of the show, often burned out on ministries built on their backs to exalt a single leader who demands submission from his or her people.

They carry a hunger for purity, for a genuine experience of the presence of God. They know that God has called them to be more than mere pew-sitters. They want to be a people making a real difference in the church and in the world.

REDEPLOYMENT

For a number of years now, I have prophesied a time when the Lord would redeploy His sheep to places that remain true to the Word, where the Holy Spirit is free to move, and where people are healed and released into their God-ordained gifts and callings. I still see that redeployment coming. In some places, this has already begun as the hunger has spread.

A time is coming when watered-down versions of faith and church won't be enough to carry believers through a troubled world. Increasing numbers of people will be crying out for more. God will begin to shift the population of the kingdom into what I have called lighthouse churches and ministries, places that shine so brightly for the kingdom of God in the darkness that people will see and be drawn like moths to a flame. Most churches and ministries that have been called in this way have experienced intense spiritual warfare. It's been difficult, especially for those located in regions of refuge, protected from the acceleration of natural disasters coming upon the world.

The hungry remnant will gather strength and continue to grow over time. I'm not saying that seeker-sensitive megachurches will collapse any time soon or that all of them are bad, but rather that a growing number of saints hunger for more, and over time, this will set the stage for a redeployment of the Lord's people.

As they seek the genuine and the pure, increasing numbers of the Lord's chosen will develop sharper discernment to differentiate between the false, shallow, or show, and the genuine. Sensing that God is about to send the genuine, they long for more and they know it's available. The hungry remnant cries out, "Is God really sending revival? We've waited. Where is it?"

THE MOVE OF GOD

I received from the Lord another word intended to protect us from despair and discouragement, and help us walk in hope and expectation. Although it could sound confrontational, it is really a love cry. He said, "I am the sovereign God. Stop calling the shots for Me. Stop presenting Me with a picture of what *you* want or expect when I move."

As both pastor and itinerant conference speaker, I've heard the voices of many discouraged and angry believers who've listened to people like me prophesying the coming of a huge move of God, a revival for this generation and this day, the great end time outpouring of the Holy Spirit. We've waited, but despite some bright spots, it seems it hasn't really manifested in fullness. Some have given up, while others just hurt. Some have actually left the church and, in some cases, even the faith. In broken faith and sometimes in anger, they bailed out.

Nevertheless, the Lord is speaking. If you want to avoid being discouraged and angry that you've cried for revival and it hasn't seemed to unfold, then surrender your idea of what it has to look like and begin focusing on what God is actually doing. Stop counting heads and looking for thousands. Stop picturing in your mind what you've read in history books or experienced in some past outpouring. Stop pining after days gone by from Azusa Street, the Jesus Movement, the Vineyard revival, the Toronto Blessing, or Brownsville/Pensacola.

We can and should learn from these past revivals—the glory, the lessons, the mistakes, and more. But God isn't recreating what was and He is not interested in undertaking old movements. As our Creator God, He has always worked to create new things and release fresh streams of water in fresh places in fresh ways. In the days to come, we'll have to surrender our own visions of what we want to see before we can truly see what God calls revival.

> WE'LL HAVE TO SURRENDER OUR OWN VISIONS OF WHAT WE WANT TO SEE BEFORE WE CAN TRULY SEE WHAT GOD CALLS REVIVAL.

If you're thinking that God isn't doing anything, you're setting yourself up as His judge, which will effectively blind you to His works and the direction in which He's moving. Begin looking for His hand in places and ways where He *is* moving, and you will find that revival, the move of the Spirit, looks a bit different than you had imagined. There may be some things about it that appear similar to what we've seen in the past... but they won't be the same. This coming move will be deeper, more settled, and more stable, more rooted in the Father's heart, more life-changing and love-filled in very visible ways. Out of it, modern day Josephs and Daniels will emerge to speak to ungodly kings and influence governments through their spiritual gifts.

Unlike many past revivals, I believe the Lord says this one—the end times revival, the great outpouring that leads to the Lord's return—comes with conditions. As a different sort of outpouring, it must have a landing pad prepared, a foundation upon which to rest. Perhaps other revivals came to lay foundations for later ones, but this coming outpouring must rest upon a stable, consistent, and pure foundation in order to take us to the return of the Lord.

AN OUTPOURING LONG PROPHESIED

The coming outpouring is consistently prophesied in both Testaments. The foundation it rests upon is made crystal clear.

> Behold, I am going to send you Elijah the prophet before the coming of the great and terrible day of the LORD. He will restore the hearts of the fathers to their children and the hearts of the children to their fathers, so that I will not come and smite the land with a curse.　　(Malachi 4:5–6)

Jeremiah 31:13–14 points in the same direction:

> "Then the virgin will rejoice in the dance, and the young men and the old, together, for I will turn their mourning into joy and will comfort them and give them joy for their sorrow. I will fill the soul of the priests with abundance, and My people will be satisfied with My goodness," declares the LORD.

With the foundation of that restoration of generational love and connection in place, God releases blessing while the curse is averted.

To prevent this from happening, a concerted demonic attack has been launched against prophetic fathers and leaders to neutralize their voices and even to take them out before their time. John Paul Jackson, Kim Clement, Jack Frost, and others have been among them. Where demonic forces failed to take them out by death, they have worked to cut off legacies by setting generations against one another. My own family suffered such an attack in the years leading to my father's passing and in the months that followed. Desiring to loose the curse and prevent us from making the impact we have been called to make as the body of Christ before the great and terrible day of the Lord—the return of Jesus—the devil moves to break the connection between generations.

As I've traveled the world, I've met too many fine servants of the Lord whose children are not serving God. Much of this has come about because of imbalance between ministry and family. Often, the children of Christian leaders pay too high a price for their parents' ministries. Much more of this has developed because of unhealed areas of the heart in both the old and the young. And it doesn't just affect leadership. Across the body of Christ, an abandoned and wounded generation leads lives of disillusionment.

> AN ABANDONED AND WOUNDED GENERATION LEADS LIVES OF DISILLUSIONMENT AND THIS GENERATIONAL BREACH HAS BEEN EXPLOITED BY THE POWERS OF DARKNESS.

This generational breach has been exploited by the powers of darkness. The remedy is repentance and sanctification that leads to healing and wholeness, forgiveness and reconciliation. We, the older generation, must make amends for failures by intentionally and persistently reaching out in love. It begins with us, not the young.

THE GREAT END TIME OUTPOURING

A powerful end time move of God is coming, but it comes with conditions. Reconciling the generations is only one of those. Revelation 14 clearly articulates several more.

> *Then I looked, and behold, the Lamb was standing on Mount Zion, and with Him one hundred and forty-four thousand, having His name and the name of His Father written on their foreheads. And I heard a voice from heaven, like the sound of many waters and like the sound of loud thunder, and the voice which I heard was like the sound of harpists playing on their harps. And they sang a new song before the throne and before the four living creatures and the elders; and no one could learn the song except the one hundred and forty-four thousand who had been purchased from the earth. These are the ones who have not been defiled with women, for they have kept themselves chaste. These are the ones who follow the Lamb wherever He goes. These have been purchased from among men as first fruits to God and to the Lamb. And no lie was found in their mouth; they are blameless. And I saw another angel flying in mid-heaven, having an eternal gospel to preach to those who live on the earth, and to every nation and tribe and tongue and people.* (Revelation 14:1–6)

Who are these one hundred and forty-four thousand? You will find a complete explanation of the symbolism in my book, *A Vision of Hope for the End Times: Why I Want to*

Be Left Behind.[2] For now, understand that the number represents the whole people of God. Twelve times twelve makes one hundred and forty-four and points to twelve patriarchs and twelve apostles. One thousand is a number symbolizing a great many.

WORSHIP AT THE DEPTHS

Through the symbolic one hundred and forty-four thousand, a new pulse of powerful and creative worship is now being, and will yet be, released, full of power and creativity. Prophetically speaking, the office of the psalmist will be wedded with the prophetic gift. Worship will take a renewed center stage in our lives as believers—fresh, alive, and pursued until the point of breakthrough into the glory and presence of God. This coming outpouring will be fueled by dedicated worshipers steeped in the presence of God.

> A GENERATION OF BELIEVERS WILL ARISE
> WHO BROOK NO COMPROMISE.

ABSOLUTE DEVOTION

Represented by the one hundred and forty-four thousand, a generation of believers will arise who brook no compromise. In Scripture, idolatry and compromised devotion to God are described as adultery committed by an unfaithful bride, thus the reference to being undefiled by women. This end time remnant company of the passionate are wholly devoted to God in every aspect of life, deeply in love with Jesus. Even now, this remnant emerges and grows in number.

---

2. R. Loren Sandford, *A Vision of Hope for the End Times: Why I Want to Be Left Behind* (Shippensburg, PA: Destiny Image, 2018).

A PEOPLE OF INTEGRITY

John wrote that no lie is found in their mouths. (See Revelation 14:5.) The end time remnant will be known for being the most reliable, most trustworthy people on the planet. As God is faithful, so will His true people be known for their faithfulness. For this reason, we have seen a rising tide of exposure of sin in leaders. Judgment has been under way to purify and separate the precious from the vile and good from evil.

THE END TIME HARVEST

Finally, the end time remnant represented by one hundred and forty-four thousand will be at the center of a great harvest of souls from every nation and ethnic group on the planet. This great ingathering and spread of the gospel of Jesus Christ will rest upon the foundation of those who have first conformed to these three conditions: worship, singular devotion, and integrity. Already I see God calling forth those who've plumbed the depths of the Spirit of Jesus and sold themselves out to God in purity. Add to all of that a movement restoring the hearts of fathers in the body of Christ to a generational connection and you have a picture of God's work in the last days.

THE HOUR OF DECISION

We live in an hour of decision, a day when holiness matters, when what you got away with in the outer court will destroy you in the inner court. Consequences will ensue if we presume to touch the holy unprepared. The clock is ticking and it's time to prepare.

PROPHETIC MINISTRY

With the emergence of the symbolic one hundred and forty-four thousand comes a reformation in prophetic ministry, a heart-level change in those who would move in the prophetic gift. Again, I say that in this hour, God moves us toward purity and holiness. True prophetic voices speak from the heart of the Father, dead to ambition and greed. Humility and love must reign.

> TRUE PROPHETIC VOICES SPEAK FROM THE HEART OF THE FATHER, DEAD TO AMBITION AND GREED. HUMILITY AND LOVE MUST REIGN.

In a time of much imbalance in what passes for prophetic ministry, our Lord is bringing balance to those who will submit and receive it. We prophetic people must do better than we have done. God is bringing up those with a fresh heart for prophetic purity so that we can, indeed, do better. Balanced prophetic ministry carries promise and warning, blessing and confrontation of wickedness, edification and conviction, encouragement and admonition. When it involves prediction, it carries a purpose to release power and love to accomplish God's goals.

An ever-widening chasm will open up between two camps in the prophetic. The positive-words-only camp and the balanced camp will increasingly stand against one another. In observing and recognizing this, it will be essential that we not fall into criticism of one another across the chasm.

THE NATION AND THE WORLD

In 2011, I prophesied verbally and in writing that we would see escalating natural disasters. Referring to my own nation, the United States, I said I was particularly concerned for the coastal states. In the ensuing years, we've seen those disasters unfold in hundred-year floods, mudslides, hurricanes, and fires. There will be more.

Climate change is real. The only debate is whether it is man-caused or part of a natural cycle. Worldwide, there will continue to be an increase in earthquakes and volcanoes affecting major population centers. My own spin on climate change and other natural disasters is that Earth can no longer bear up under the accumulated sin of mankind and now reacts to it. The damaging effects of climate change will impact many nations around the world.

> *For the anxious longing of the creation waits eagerly for the revealing of the sons of God.* (Romans 8:19)

In Matthew 24, Jesus Himself spoke of an end time escalation of natural disasters:

> *For nation will rise against nation, and kingdom against kingdom, and in various places there will be famines and earthquakes. But all these things are merely the beginning of birth pangs.* (Matthew 24:7–8)

Earth travails to give birth to the coming kingdom of God.

In all of this, there will be what I call regions of refuge, places of relative safety from the disasters occurring elsewhere. Spiritual warfare over these regions has been intense because the Lord wants lighthouse churches and ministries moving in the Holy Spirit to be available for those in disaster-prone areas. These regions of refuge include the Front Range of Colorado, where I live, and the panhandle of Idaho and western Montana. These are merely two examples. Masses of people have already moved to these two regions, dramatically expanding their populations. People may give many reasons for moving, but God has a divine purpose in it.

I've observed something that may not hold true in all cases. Many of the regions where bursts of revival have already broken out are places I see and feel are at greater risk for these natural disasters. Spiritual warfare doesn't rage so heavily there because not so much is at stake as in regions of refuge. This might be a controversial statement, but it is an observation I've made.

If I'm right, this places a significant weight of responsibility on churches and ministries in regions of refuge, wherever they may be, to be embassies of the kingdom of God. In any embassy, the laws of the nation it represents prevail because the ground on which the embassy sits becomes that nation's soil. Wherever our fellowships meet therefore becomes holy ground, the territory of the kingdom of God where kingdom law prevails.

Clearly, people have been flocking to regions I see as regions of refuge. Often, they don't even know why, but I'm telling you that God is sending them and we need to be ready to receive them.

PARTING WORDS

When praying for these coming days, and as I've prayed for the great end time outpouring of the Spirit and the brightness of our rising in a time of darkness over the nations (see Isaiah 60), I see a vision of little bits and pieces, like straw, blowing in the wind. I sense that the revival we long for will not come with a big bang or a crash, but will come together as little pieces blowing in the wind of His Spirit coalesce into something much larger. If you fail to seize upon the little bits, however, and focus on what God is doing a piece at a time, you'll miss it. Jesus said, *"The wind blows where it wishes and you hear the sound of it, but do not know where it comes from and where it is going; so is everyone who is born of the Spirit"* (John 3:8).

> THE REVIVAL WE LONG FOR WILL COME TOGETHER AS LITTLE PIECES BLOWING IN THE WIND OF HIS SPIRIT COALESCE INTO SOMETHING MUCH LARGER.

We live in a time like that. The wind blows and we don't really know where it's coming from or where it goes, but we need to be alert and yielded to catch the breeze as it carries all the little pieces that add up to glory.

A TIME FOR MAGNIFIED PRAYERS

I'm not speaking figuratively when I say that we live in the time John prophesied in Revelation 8:3–5:

> *Another angel came and stood at the altar, holding a golden censer; and much incense was given to him, so that he might add it to the prayers of all the saints on the golden altar which was before the throne. And the smoke of the incense, with the prayers of the saints, went up before God out of the angel's hand. Then the angel took the censer and filled it with the fire of the altar, and threw it to the earth; and there followed peals of thunder and sounds and flashes of lightning and an earthquake.*

The season of prayer magnified in heaven is now. The fire of the kingdom of God will be cast into the earth in response. I've prophesied this for a number of years, but prophetic people often see and live ahead of the fulfillment of their words. Now is the time I've long waited to see. In my own church, our corporate prayer times have been growing in both numbers and power, just as they are in many other places. I see these verses from Revelation 8 unfolding now in real time. Supernaturally magnified prayer and intercession form the foundation of everything else I've said in this chapter.

7

WHEN GOD'S JUDGMENT IS COMPASSION

For a long time now, I've carried a growing burden for holiness, a word too often misunderstood and misapplied. The impression usually seems to be that holiness means avoiding a particular set of activities and having no fun, as if we could be condemned into behaving in certain ways religion deems *good*. In the process, God gets a bad rap, while the truth is so very different than that. First, *holy* means to be set aside for a specific purpose. Holy things must not be used for any purposes other than those for which they have been designated. We have been set aside to be with Him, to know Him, to rest in Him, to sense Him, and to represent Him.

Holiness therefore means joy, laughter, good friends, good food, and great sex in the marriage bed. Occasionally, it means fasting when a cleansing is needed, when seeking a fresh revelation, or when you need to solidify a repentance of some kind—but that's not the focus. At its core, holiness represents God accurately and with integrity. The true nature of God is a wonderful thing!

> YOU WHO HAVE RECEIVED JESUS ARE ALREADY HOLY, NO MATTER WHAT YOU MIGHT THINK OF YOURSELF, YOUR FAILURES, OR YOUR INWARD THOUGHTS.

In the sense that you have been set aside for God's exclusive purposes, you who have received Jesus are already holy, no matter what you might think of yourself, your failures, or your inward thoughts. In fact, you will never be more holy or more set apart than you are at this moment. Jesus made you holy. He accepted you as His own and set you apart from the rest of the world. He cleansed you when He died on that cross and rose from the dead. You're His. This enabled the apostle Paul to write Colossians 3:12–14:

> *So, as those who have been chosen of God, holy and beloved, put on a heart of compassion, kindness, humility, gentleness and patience; bearing with one another, and forgiving each other, whoever has a complaint against anyone; just as the Lord forgave you, so also should you. Beyond all these things put on love, which is the perfect bond of unity.*

Because we have been made holy and set apart, God appeals to us to live like holy people.

Let our relationships reflect the way holy people relate to one another. Let us truly be different than the world around us. Let every word and action reflect His nature.

First Corinthians 6:9–11 reads:

Or do you not know that the unrighteous will not inherit the kingdom of God? Do not be deceived; neither fornicators, nor idolaters, nor adulterers, nor effeminate, nor homosexuals, nor thieves, nor the covetous, nor drunkards, nor revilers, nor swindlers, will inherit the kingdom of God. Such were some of you; but you were washed, but you were sanctified, but you were justified in the name of the Lord Jesus Christ and in the Spirit of our God.

"Sanctified" means you were set apart, made holy, when you received Jesus. It's done. *"Such **were** some of you."* Past tense. Since receiving Jesus, you are no longer those unholy things by identity. By identity, you ceased to be *sinner* and became *saint*. Holy behavior must follow after holy identity. Paul's plea was that we all would live day to day in accord with the new identity we have been given.

HOLINESS AND JUDGMENT

This leads to the issue of judgment. Holiness and judgment come hand in hand. God is more than just our Father. He's also the righteous Judge, and as such, He will deal with evil, sin, and immorality because He must. But what does that mean?

> GOD IS MORE THAN JUST OUR FATHER.
> HE'S ALSO THE RIGHTEOUS JUDGE.

People tend to go to one of two extremes when talking about judgment. One extreme is the condemnation side: legalistic, condemning, and often angry. "God will judge and punish you for breaking His rules so you'd better look out." When talking about the nation, we hear that God will judge and destroy

America for its sin, or, "All those evil abortionists and those liberal politicians and lawbreakers and all the rest will suffer under the wrath of God!" I have no quarrel with any of that, except that, by itself, it's one-sided and unbalanced.

The other extreme is often called *hyper-grace*. The hyper-grace side says sin and evil are all covered. We're not under the Law anymore, so we're free and there's no condemnation for anything we do. Say the magical sinner's prayer and you're automatically going to heaven, regardless of what kind of life you've lived.

The judgment side validly understands that God is the Judge and King who hands down laws and expects to be obeyed. The extreme grace side thinks that the cross somehow absolved all of that in such a way that we no longer have to live under God's laws because grace covers it. No consequences!

So it's either a presentation of God as the big angry Judge up there just itching to punish sinners, or the gentle permissive Father who lets His kids do whatever they want, whether or not it's good for them. One is the outraged God and the other is the indulgent God. Is God angry? Or does His love mean He is never angry? Is God angry with *you*? Does grace mean that the nature of God has changed from one testament to the other?

GOD'S ANGER

Scripture clearly presents God as capable of anger. Why does God experience anger? What provokes Him? Is it because we broke the rules…or is it because when we break the rules, we do damage to ourselves and to others? Could it be that God, in His love, reacts to the damage we do, sometimes even in anger? God experiences and acts in anger precisely *because* He loves, not because He's a control freak who just wants to impose meaningless rules on us so that He can punish us when we cross the line.

I have three children, all grown. When they were still under my roof, I was never angry with them simply over loss of control over them. My anger grew from the knowledge that if they continued in what they were doing, their lives would be wrecked and people would be hurt. I didn't want that. I, however, am just a broken human being. God is better than I was, am, or ever could be. He loves more powerfully and consistently than I ever could. He's perfect in it. I'm not.

> **WHEN GOD'S ANGRY, IT'S NOT ABOUT HIM.**
> **IT'S ABOUT THE DAMAGE WE'RE DOING TO OURSELVES.**

So, there's selfish anger and there's godly anger that flows from love. Healthy and righteous anger can erupt for the sake of someone you love. That's our God. When He's angry, it's not about Him. It's about the damage we're doing to ourselves. That damage offends Him and leads Him to move to end it—hence, the cross, and the consistent call of Scripture to repentance, sanctification, and holiness.

Psalm 135:14 asserts, *"For the LORD will judge His people and will have compassion on His servants."* Hebrew poetry, as we see it in the Psalms, rhymes thoughts and concepts in parallelism. Most often, it's the same thought expressed in different ways. Sometimes, it's contrasting thoughts written in parallel. In English poetry, by contrast, we rhyme sounds, as in, "Roses are red and violets are blue. Great and awesome is my love for you." Sorry for the cheap poetry, but it illustrates the point. In the case of Psalm 135:14, because of parallelism, God's judgment and God's compassion are so intertwined as to be nearly indistinguishable. God judges because He loves. In fact, His judgment expresses His love. *"For the LORD will judge His people and will have compassion on His servants."*

Judgment does not equate with punishment. Punishment can never produce righteousness. Punishment destroys. Judgment is something else, something better.

In the New Testament, the word group for *judgment* means to cut or separate, decisions rendered to separate good from evil. God's judgment first reveals, weighs, sorts, and separates the clean from the unclean. In that light, we should regard judgment as a gift of love rather than a punishment. God renders and executes judgment for our good, not for destruction or harm. Ultimately, it flows from God's heart of compassion. Sin kills and destroys. Sin produces suffering and breaks relationships. It damages us at the core of our humanity. God therefore moves to end the destruction and bring us to a better way.

> GOD RENDERS AND EXECUTES JUDGMENT FOR OUR GOOD.
> ULTIMATELY, IT FLOWS FROM GOD'S HEART OF COMPASSION.

CONTEMPORARY CULTURE

Look at the culture of our day. As we've abandoned and rejected God's moral principles, a devastating wave of hatred has been loosed in the land. We're tearing ourselves apart as a nation. As we move more deeply into the post-Christian era, the same destruction now engulfs other nations and other cultures. In the United States, we see mass killings in our schools and workplaces. Americans have had the right to bear arms since our nation's inception, but it hasn't been until recent years that we have seen these massacres. The problem, therefore, has never been guns. The problem is the deterioration of society that results from writing God out of public life and culture. This rising wave of hatred has produced riots in our streets and a Congress so paralyzed with hatred that it can't get anything done.

God hates suffering and division as offenses to His love. Unclean attitudes, thoughts, judgments, and emotions defile us and make life heavy and unhappy. God didn't create us for that. He made us for joy, fulfillment, and peace.

> Let the wicked forsake his way and the unrighteous man his thoughts; and let him return to the LORD, and He will have compassion on him, and to our God, for He will abundantly pardon. "For My thoughts are not your thoughts, nor are your ways My ways," declares the LORD. "For as the heavens are higher than the earth, so are My ways higher than your ways and My thoughts than your thoughts."
>
> (Isaiah 55:7–9)

In judgment, God acts to cleanse and realign us with His ways so that we don't have to suffer, so that we don't make messes in our families and relationships, so that we don't damage ourselves, and so that we live well and in peace.

> For the word of God is living and active and sharper than any two-edged sword, and piercing as far as the division of soul and spirit, of both joints and marrow, and able to **judge** the thoughts and intentions of the heart. And there is no creature hidden from His sight, but all things are open and laid bare to the eyes of Him with whom we have to do.
>
> (Hebrews 4:12–13)

GOD EXPOSES THE UNCLEAN IN ORDER TO WEIGH, EVALUATE, AND SEPARATE OUT WHAT IS NOT CLEAN IN OUR THOUGHTS AND INTENTIONS, UNTIL THEY ALIGN WITH HIS.

God exposes the unclean in order to weigh, evaluate, and separate out what is not clean in our thoughts and intentions, until our thoughts and intentions align with His. Judgment exposes and reveals the truth of our inner selves, our cultures, and our nations. We serve a God who loves us enough to do this. If we choose to receive it, we will reap the benefit. We have come into a crucial period of history in which holiness matters, perhaps as it never has before in our lifetimes.

THE DISCIPLINE OF THE LORD

Unfortunately, holiness has become an unpopular word today, even in Christian circles. God's discipline for the purpose of holiness holds little appeal for a culture steeped in comfort. The author of Hebrews wrote:

> *You have not yet resisted to the point of shedding blood in your striving against sin; and you have forgotten the exhortation which is addressed to you as sons, "My son, do not regard lightly the discipline of the Lord, nor faint when you are reproved by Him; for those whom the Lord loves He disciplines, and He scourges every son whom He receives." It is for discipline that you endure; God deals with you as with sons; for what son is there whom his father does not discipline? But if you are without discipline, of which all have become partakers, then you are illegitimate children and not sons. Furthermore, we had earthly fathers to discipline us, and we respected them; shall we not much rather be subject to the Father of spirits, and live? For they disciplined us for a short time as seemed best to them, but He disciplines us for our good, so that we may share His holiness. All discipline for the moment seems not to be joyful, but sorrowful; yet to those who have been trained by it, afterwards it yields the peaceful fruit of righteousness.* (Hebrews 12:4–11)

This Scripture embodies the essence of God's heart for us in His judgment. *"He disciplines us for our good so that we may share His holiness."* This reflects Proverbs 22:15: *"Foolishness is bound up in the heart of a child; the rod of discipline will remove it far from him."* Judgment separates the good from the bad and establishes the good. Our Father God loves us enough to do what it takes to remove foolishness from us so that nothing unclean or defiling remains, nothing broken, and nothing to do damage.

Hebrews 12 speaks of *"the peaceful fruit of righteousness."* When you've been trained by God's discipline, and have come under His judgment in love, you can rest in what has been established in you and live well and free. For instance, when God's discipline and judgment have done their work, recovering addicts no longer struggle with temptation because sobriety has now become an established element of character. Peace reigns. When the peaceful fruit of righteousness has been implanted, it's no longer a decision not to pick up that joint or take that drink or pop that pill. Those temptations have been removed. Sobriety is now who you've become. Peaceful fruit.

The discipline of the Lord that sorts good from evil and drives out foolishness will make you an honest person incapable of compromise where integrity is concerned. When you have income that the Internal Revenue Service, the U.S. tax collection agency, would never know about, you report it without a second thought—with no struggle or guilt, just peace—because integrity is who you are and what you've become. As a result, you sow nothing into the spirit realm that you will have to reap later. You are who you are when people are looking, and you are who you are when they are not.

I know that I will never commit adultery or even experience real temptation from a woman who is not my wife. God's discipline on my life in that area began when I was young and has established something in my heart and character that I can rest in; there's no temptation to struggle with. It's the peaceful fruit of established righteousness. Faithfulness to my wife is a settled element of character.

I pray, "Treat me as a son, Father God. Let Your discipline shape me for my own good and for the good of Your kingdom." I want no uncleanness in me. I know that I will never be perfect until the Lord Himself perfects me in eternity, but in this life, I long to grow in holiness, both for the sake of a peaceful life and for the sake of the kingdom of God, the glory of my Lord.

THE LAST DAYS

We live in a time when holiness matters as never before. I believe these are the last days and that what happens now carries more weight than at any other time in my life, and perhaps in history.

Jesus promised in John 14:12–13:

> *Truly, truly, I say to you, he who believes in Me, the works that I do, he will do also; and greater works than these he will do; because I go to the Father. Whatever you ask in My name, that will I do, so that the Father may be glorified in the Son.*

At some point soon, we will receive an outpouring of the Holy Spirit at a level of power not seen since the day of Pentecost, when the Holy Spirit was first released on the people of God. God never intended, however, that we should exercise His power without solid grounding in holy character, but neither did He intend that we should walk in holy character without exercising His power. Holy character is the visible demonstration of who He is in you or me. It's what makes you or me trustworthy. It is the platform that carries the perfect love that flows from the heart of God.

> ## HOLY CHARACTER IS THE VISIBLE DEMONSTRATION OF WHO GOD IS IN YOU OR ME.

God appointed power, miracles, and healing to be the demonstration of who He is to the world. These things validate the reality of His kingdom come to earth and give tangible substance to His love. At that point, the gospel becomes more than a theology, more than an idea. It becomes visible reality. Sustaining the ministry of power requires a foundation in character and wholeness. On the other hand, without the power, I'm not sure we can sustain the character. One feeds the other.

TIMES OF EXPOSURE

I have long prophesied that the time would come when things you got away with in the outer court in previous years would get you killed in the inner court where we're going. Deeper levels of intimacy in the raw presence of God lie before us. Because of this, we live in a time of exposure when the judgment of God is wedded with the compassion and mercy of God, as the psalmist wrote. (See, for example, Psalm 89.) We therefore see accelerating exposure in the church, in our private lives, in government, in society, and in business.

There was a time—and I lived through it—when people could lead immoral lives or harbor hidden compromise, walking in lapses of integrity, and continue to minister the power of God. There was a time when leaders could lead in abusive ways, exploiting the flock of God for personal gain, dominating and controlling people, building personal cultish followings, and still God would bless. Miracles would happen and manifestations of the Spirit would be seen. Thousands would come to their meetings and God would show up in power. But then the exposures began to come. Sin was uncovered. Leaders began to fall, their hidden corruption revealed for all the world to see.

People began to ask me how God could pour out His miracles through such defiled vessels. Why would He do that? I answered by saying that anointing has never been, and never will be, a measure of God's approval. King Saul was the Lord's anointed even after falling into disobedience. Judas, the Lord's betrayer, spent three and a half years ministering power with the other disciples, healing the sick, raising the dead, and casting out demons, and yet he became one of history's greatest and most tragic failures. God doesn't hold His love hostage to the condition of the one who ministers. He heals because He loves people, not because of who stands on the platform. It's about people, not the vessel through whom God pours His love.

The time has ended, however, when spiritual leaders are allowed to get away with hidden sin, year after year, and continue to walk in the power of God. He is bringing about a balance of holy character with demonstrations of power and healing. Those who walk in power with a flawed foundation in character are being exposed and disciplined, one after another. Every time one of those falls, however, the world sees it, the name of Jesus is dishonored, the church is discredited, and the gospel becomes harder for outsiders to believe. In kindness and love, God therefore says, "*The LORD will judge His people and will have compassion on His servants*" (Psalm 135:14).

This sifting, sorting, exposing, and refining expresses His compassion for the suffering we bring upon ourselves and upon others in our brokenness. These correctives come for our healing and from God's need to preserve His own reputation, glory, and honor. I believe the name of Jesus suffers dishonor every time some moral failing in a leader is exposed before the world, but I also believe the name of Jesus is dishonored everywhere His people fail to walk in His kingdom power, for whatever reasons that may be.

His discipline and His judgment, therefore, come from a heart of love. I pray with the psalmist:

Let my judgment come forth from Your presence; let Your eyes look with equity. You have tried my heart; You have visited me by night; You have tested me and You find nothing; I have purposed that my mouth will not transgress.

(Psalm 17:2–3)

THE NEED FOR INNER HEALING

I want nothing to do with any form of cheap grace that allows me to merely continue as I have before. I long for the true grace that changes me and holds me accountable. Judge me, Lord, sort me out. Separate the precious from the vile.

As I pray this, I'm not just talking about the obvious sins. I'm also referring to the things we deal with in what we often call *inner healing* or *inner transformation*, the brokenness we live with at the level of the heart and the wounds and fears that lie hidden inside of us to spring up and defile our lives.

Recently, some top leaders in renewal circles have denied the need for inner healing. These are good people making an impact for the kingdom of God, but they're missing something. Such statements usually reveal ignorance of what inner healing truly is, or they stem from exposure to unbiblical approaches to inner healing ministry.

The term *inner healing* came about during the charismatic renewal that touched the mainline denominations and other groups during the 1960s and '70s. People who had never experienced the reality of the Holy Spirit before were getting excited about the idea that Jesus was real and that He could heal the physical body. That led to the realization that He could heal the wounded heart as well. Thus was born the term *inner healing*. A few intrepid pioneers began to study the Word while observing people, until real fruit began to be borne in the lives of those to whom they ministered in areas that had once been strongholds of brokenness.

Although the etymology of the term is understandable, it is inaccurate, and perhaps misleading. A better definition is embedded in Romans 12:2: *"Be transformed by the renewing of your mind."* The key word is *transformed*, meaning that we must be changed into the image of the Son. (See Romans 8:29.) The *mind* in the culture of the Bible is not just what you think between your ears. It's the whole inner self—thoughts, inclinations, emotions, orientation toward life, and so on. The language of Romans 12:2 clearly suggests that this transformation is not a done deal in this life, but rather something to be pursued.

> REAL INNER HEALING IS BASED IN THE CROSS
> WHERE WE DIE WITH CHRIST.

Real inner healing is based in the cross where we die with Christ. Repentance and forgiveness, both for others and self, and, yes, healing, are central. The primary purpose of all of this is not that we should merely be happy, but to free us to be more effectively given away in the power of the Holy Spirit for the sake of the Lord, others and the kingdom of God, conforming to the image of the Son.

Jesus tells us, *"Whoever wishes to save his life will lose it, but whoever loses his life for My sake and the gospel's will save it"*

(Mark 8:35). I have said to some audiences that the wonderful personal ministry going on in the meeting is for them, but not about them. It is, rather, to prepare them for the coming move of God, which is not focused on self, but on changing nations. For this reason, inner healing is about growing in the holiness we've already been given and removing obstacles to that growth.

> **THE CRY FROM HEAVEN IS THAT POWER AND LOVE MUST REST ON A SOLID FOUNDATION OF GODLINESS AND INTEGRITY REFLECTIVE OF THE FATHER'S HEART.**

The cry from heaven in our day—the core message that is both a promise of blessing and a warning not to be ignored—is that power and love, the kingdom of God come to earth, must rest on a solid foundation of godliness and integrity reflective of the Father's heart. It would therefore be wise to seek and embrace God's judgment that sorts the good from the bad, the impure from the pure, and to know that this is God's compassion and love.

This kind of judgment must not be confused with the punishment Jesus already took on our behalf when He went to the cross. Because of what He did for us, we are holy and set apart, as set apart as we will ever be. We are special, chosen, and glorious, but we are also in the process of being sifted and sorted to become more glorious, more effective, and more filled with joy. We are being changed from glory to glory as we gaze into who Jesus is and as the light of His presence exposes, cleanses, and transforms us.

8

LOVE, HONOR, AND WATERMELON FOOTBALL

God has never been interested in merely getting people saved so they can go to heaven. Jesus's message is that the kingdom of God has come to earth. While we have been well taught that the kingdom brings relief from suffering, and that signs, wonders, and healings happen, I believe we've often missed a key component. The kingdom of God is a culture of light and love. Imagine the actual culture of the kingdom of God manifest on earth! As we prepare for a coming move of God, wouldn't it be wise to plumb the depths of the form of love we call honor?

A CULTURE OF HONOR

Never should we underestimate the function and power of culture. The culture in which we live conditions the way we think, feel, and behave at levels and at depths of which we are seldom aware. For instance, in the United States, over the course of several centuries, culture conditioned people to think of black people as inferior and less intelligent. This seemed to them to be self-evident. It was, of course, a lie, but cultural conditioning made it seem real. I have encountered Asian cultures that condition people to extreme performance orientation and even aggressive behavior. This seems normal to them, the right way to live. Culture teaches us how to feel and think, how to speak, how to dress, and what constitutes acceptable behavior. It's the soup in which we live.

But what if we in the church lived and moved in a true culture of light? What if the culture of heaven so conditioned all who became part of it that forgiveness was second nature to them? No struggle. No decision to make. What if a culture of the kingdom taught us to engage in self-sacrifice for others as a means to real joy? And what if that became simply the way we live and relate to life? What if the heart of our culture in the body of Christ was about real love of the sort Jesus poured out? *What if…?*

At the core of such a culture lies the issue of honor—not honor received, but honor rendered. In recent years, among Christians hungry for renewal and revival, we've heard a lot of talk about a culture of honor. In fact, you'd be hard-pressed to find any church or any individual Christian anywhere in renewal circles these days not talking about love and honor. Ask them! What is church about? They'll tell you that it's all about love and honor! But in actual practice, is that really what characterizes our culture?

> LOVE WITHOUT THE GIFT OF HONOR IS NOT LOVE,
> AND HONOR WITHOUT LOVE IS A SHAM.

Love and honor are interlinked. Never does one exist without the other. Love without the gift of honor is not love, and honor without love is a sham, just a collection of meaningless words.

WATERMELON FOOTBALL

Have you ever tried to play American-style watermelon football? I dreamed up that game when I served as a youth pastor in the mid-1970s, looking for fun things to do at a youth group picnic. It was hilarious! The poor melon lasted only about two plays before somebody dropped and broke it. At that point, the players just tried to use the largest of the remaining pieces because every play meant it broke into yet smaller pieces. Messy business! Once the watermelon broke, the juice made it wet and slippery so that hanging on to it became a challenge. Before the game was over, everyone was a sticky mess, and nobody ever made a touchdown with a whole melon.

The truth is that maintaining love and a culture of honor in the body of Christ is a lot like playing watermelon football—hard to grip and even more difficult to retain in one piece. It keeps slipping away. We grasp it for a while, the team advances for a few months or years, and then it gets messy. Somebody drops it, it breaks, and you try to move forward with whatever is left of the larger pieces.

From the time the church was born on the day of Pentecost almost two thousand years ago, Christians have been playing watermelon football with the culture of love and honor. We just can't seem to hang on to it long enough to cross the goal line with the whole thing intact.

Had the early church been able to maintain it, the New Testament would likely contain only the four Gospels, the book of Acts, the Revelation to John, most of Romans, and fragments of Paul's other letters. Paul, James, and Peter all wrote their letters to correct problems infecting the churches. Some of those threats were doctrinal, but a distressing number of them were relational. Bitterness. Conflicts. Divisions. Judgments on one another. Dishonor of leaders. The need to forgive and come together as one.

THE FIRST CONFLICT

The church couldn't have been but a few weeks old when an ethnic conflict had already erupted.

> Now at this time while the disciples were increasing in number, a complaint arose on the part of the Hellenistic Jews against the native Hebrews, because their widows were being overlooked in the daily serving of food.   (Acts 6:1)

The Jews who were native to Judea were being accused of prejudice toward the Jews who had come to Jerusalem from the Greek-speaking world, conditioned by the culture of the Greeks. Even in the atmosphere of overpowering love reported in the last half of Acts 2, they nearly dropped the watermelon.

Rather than permit division, however, they overcame the failings in their attitudes and crafted a solution to keep love flowing by appointing a team of deacons to oversee the welfare program and ensure that things were done with fairness and equity.

AN APOSTOLIC FAILURE

Here's one, however, that didn't turn out so well. Paul, while he was still called Saul, wanted to take a second missionary journey with his partner Barnabas to check up on the churches they'd planted. Conflict erupted.

Barnabas wanted to take John, called Mark, along with them also. But Paul kept insisting that they should not take him along who had deserted them in Pamphylia and had not gone with them to the work. And there occurred such a sharp disagreement that they separated from one another, and Barnabas took Mark with him and sailed away to Cyprus. (Acts 15:37–39)

> ## WHAT GREATER GLORY MIGHT HAVE UNFOLDED IF PAUL AND BARNABAS HAD STOOD TOGETHER IN UNITY?

In a failure of love and honor, they dropped the watermelon, it broke, and Paul took the larger piece. Apparently, Paul still had a bit of the Pharisee in him—rigidly judgmental and perhaps more than a bit self-righteous. What greater glory might have unfolded if Paul and Barnabas had stood together in unity? How much more effective might they have been had Paul been able to honor young John Mark, even in the latter's weakness? Later on, in 2 Timothy, the apostle wrote that Mark was very useful to him and he wanted Mark to come to him. By that time, thank God, Paul's heart had softened and he'd learned a thing or two about grace, love, and what it means to honor one another, even in failure.

THE CULTURE OF HONOR

The culture of honor—a culture of love—is so much more than just saying only nice things about one another or giving others place and position. It goes well beyond simply building one another up. These things are necessary and a number of churches have encouraged, preached, and tried to practice them, but if that's all there is, then it all becomes an empty exercise devoid of real meaning and impact. It becomes nothing more than nice-sounding words. The test comes and reality impacts us at the point where we make mistakes and offend one another. Our words come out wrong and we say the wrong things in the wrong ways. The proverbial rubber hits the road when anger runs away with us and we wound others with our expression of it.

Knowing all this, Jesus repeatedly said things like, *"For if you forgive others for their transgressions, your heavenly Father will also forgive you. But if you do not forgive others, then your Father will not forgive your transgressions"* (Matthew 6:14–15).

Then came Matthew 18:21–22:

Then Peter came and said to Him, "Lord, how often shall my brother sin against me and I forgive him? Up to seven times?" Jesus said to him, "I do not say to you, up to seven times, but up to seventy times seven."

Jesus repeated that answer in a different form in Luke 17.

In the verses following the parable of the slave whose master forgave him an enormous debt, but the slave refused to forgive others their debt, Matthew 18:34–35 says this:

And his lord, moved with anger, handed him over to the torturers until he should repay all that was owed him. My heavenly Father will also do the same to you, if each of you does not forgive his brother from your heart.

In 1 Corinthians 11, Paul rebuked the Corinthian church for the selfish and insensitive manner in which they celebrated their love feasts and partook of communion. He called them out for their disunity, their failure to honor one another, rich or poor, and their lack of love. Some in Corinth regarded themselves as better than others because of the spiritual gifts they moved in.

Again, the apostle confronted them. Later in 1 Corinthians 13, he told them that love isn't love until it is patient, kind, and not jealous of another's place, position, or blessing.

Love isn't love until it isn't arrogant, until we're no longer exalting ourselves over others, no longer focused on our own hurt or vindication, wealth, place, or position.

Love isn't love until we can no longer be provoked into anger or actions that tear others down in anger. Accordingly, love isn't love until we refuse to take into account wrongs suffered and choose to render ourselves immune to feeding on past offenses, until we stop rehearsing them in our minds over and over again.

> LOVE BECOMES REAL ONLY WHEN IT BEARS ALL THINGS,
> WHEN I WILL WALK WITH YOU NO MATTER WHAT YOU DO.

Love becomes real only when it bears all things. I will walk with you no matter what you do, whether or not you ever change. In the spirit of that commitment, love hopes all things. This requires that I see the best in you and feed on that vision for the future. I'll put up with all of your failings and love you through them, enduring all things.

This constitutes the heart of a culture of honor. This is the whole watermelon we want to carry across the goal line. The apostle Paul filled his letters with exhortations to honor in the face of failure or offense. Absent such a gift of grace, there can be no culture of honor. Without it, all that remains is a culture of performance in which we honor only those we deem worthy, while we distance ourselves from those we deem unworthy. This is neither the vision Jesus had in mind, nor is it the kingdom of God.

LOVE COVERS

Here's the apostle Paul again: *"But if any has caused sorrow, he has caused sorrow not to me, but in some degree—in order not to say too much—to all of you"* (2 Corinthians 2:5). He was saying, "I'm not going to say too much about this because it would sow something I don't want to sow. It would be a pollution and undermine the culture we're called to walk in. I'd rather cover my brother's sin than rehearse the pain in your hearing."

He continued in 2:6: *"Sufficient for such a one is this punishment which was inflicted by the majority."* His point was that some form of discipline was necessary because someone crossed the line in some way, but it was enough. It was time to let it go for the sake of mercy.

He drove home the point in 2:7: *"So that on the contrary you should rather forgive and comfort him, otherwise such a one might be overwhelmed by excessive sorrow."* The apostle was telling the Corinthian church that if they failed to forgive, and if they failed to comfort the one who offended after he had been disciplined and suffered the natural consequences of his offense, then they would only drive him down and destroy the goodness of God in him.

Don't drop the watermelon. This culture of love and honor is a fragile thing. We want to reach the goal line and make that glorious touchdown, not with just a fragment of the ball we carry, but with the whole thing intact.

THE RIGHT TO BE WRONG

Honor means that we give one another the right to be wrong, to misstate things from time to time, to act out stupidly in ways that perhaps cause wounding. Now and again, we'll draw wrong conclusions about one another and misunderstand one another, but in a true culture of love and honor, we forgive and bless when those things happen. The culture of honor thrives on forgiveness and forbearance. Without these, we will never walk in a culture of honor, but rather a culture of performance in which we honor only those we deem worthy.

> Let all bitterness and wrath and anger and clamor and slander be put away from you, along with all malice. Be kind to one another, tender-hearted, forgiving each other, just as God in Christ also has forgiven you.
>
> (Ephesians 4:31–32)

Therein lies the heart of the culture of honor. It's what Paul refused to grant John Mark and Barnabas at the beginning when he couldn't find it in his heart to give a young man the grace to fail. He could not, or would not, look past John Mark's weakness to see and call forth what John Mark would eventually become. It's what the disciples failed to give one another when they fought over who would be first and greatest in God's kingdom and then took offense at one another over it. (See Luke 9:46; 22:24; Mark 9:33–34.)

When once we step away from this grace aspect of the culture of honor, all of our perceptions of one another, our words and actions, will begin to be distorted and grow into manifestations of ugliness. We'll twist and misinterpret words and intentions and we'll drop the watermelon, imprison one another in our judgements and opinions, and fail to cross the goal line. Everything we've worked for will be destroyed.

We won't be able to hear what others are really saying. We won't perceive who they really are, and we'll take offense. We'll build cases about one another, and those cases will feed on themselves as one misperception after another builds up, passed through the filter of every misperception that came before it, each one falsely confirming the previous one. The watermelon of the culture of love and honor is a fragile thing that must be handled carefully.

> JESUS HONORED AND FORGAVE TWELVE FOOLS ON A DAILY BASIS.
> HE PUT UP WITH THEIR FAITHLESSNESS, SELFISHNESS,
> AMBITIONS, AND CONFLICTS.

Does honor therefore begin with saying only nice things about one another and giving place and position, or does it begin with grace, forgiveness, and forbearance? Jesus honored and forgave twelve fools on a daily basis. He put up with their faithlessness, their selfishness, and their ambitions and conflicts, loving them through all of it, confronting and rebuking when necessary, but honoring and favoring them. He honored them by giving them authority and sending them out on missionary journeys to minister the power of the kingdom of God, healing and casting out demons in His name. The things most precious to Him, He entrusted to that cluster of block-heads. No matter how often they failed, He honored them by bringing them into His intimate counsel and calling them His friends.

COVERING ONE ANOTHER'S NAKEDNESS

In his letters, the apostle Paul therefore spent a lot of time trying to silence talk, gossip, and criticism passed from mouth to mouth and ear to ear in the churches. Why?

Because if we ever miss this part of the culture of honor, we'll become like one of Noah's sons who exposed the naked-ness of their father.

Bear with me while I draw a metaphor from this Bible story. I'll share it as a parable or a principle of God, an illustration of the way the universe functions when honor is granted or violated. In this story, Noah, his sons, and their families have come through the flood and out of the ark. Life has begun again.

Then Noah began farming and planted a vineyard. He drank of the wine and became drunk, and uncovered himself inside his tent. Ham, the father of Canaan, saw the nakedness of his father, and told his two brothers outside. But Shem and Japheth took a garment and laid it upon both their shoulders and walked backward and covered the nakedness of their father; and their faces were turned away, so that they did not see their father's nakedness. When Noah awoke from his wine, he knew what his youngest son had done to him. So he said, "Cursed be Canaan; a servant of servants he shall be to his brothers." He also said, "Blessed be the LORD, the God of Shem; and let Canaan be his servant. May God enlarge Japheth, and let him dwell in the tents of Shem; and let Canaan be his servant."

(Genesis 9:20–27)

Granted, Noah failed; he went on a drunken binge, lost control, and dishonored himself. It was a crazy failure for a man who had done so much in obedience to God, building an ark, years in the making, while certainly taking heat from people who thought he was out of his mind. And then this failure, this disgrace.

In the New Testament, Peter wrote, *"Above all, keep fervent in your love for one another, because love covers a multitude of sins"* (1 Peter 4:8). Old or New Testament, in a culture of honor, we cover the nakedness of our brothers and sisters—the failures, the flaws, the mistakes, the transgressions, the careless words, and the hurtful actions. In a culture of honor, you don't expose one another's failures to everyone else. It doesn't pass from mouth to mouth. When failures are passed around, poison grows and love dies. Revival can neither come nor thrive.

To expose someone else's shame, failures, and flaws is to activate a curse that robs us of authority at a time when God seeks to give us an outpouring of *His* authority. When Ham exposed his father's nakedness, he brought a curse upon himself and his descendants that removed authority from them so that they became servants and slaves.

> ## IN A CULTURE OF HONOR, WE MIGHT CONFRONT A BROTHER OR SISTER IN LOVE, BUT WE DON'T EXPOSE THEIR FAULTS TO THE WORLD.

Much of the church in America—millions of Christians—remain relatively powerless and ineffective because they haven't learned what Shem and Japheth knew about covering and honoring. In a culture of honor, we might confront a brother or sister in love; we don't ignore failure or sin, but we don't expose their faults to the world either. We don't discuss it among ourselves, pass it around, and feed negativity.

A culture of honor doesn't ignore failings, but rather forgives, covers, and gives grace. This is why Jesus gave instructions on how to confront a brother or a sister in love when caught in sin. Matthew 18:15 and the following verses mandate that we first speak one on one. When that fails to produce repentance, then go with two or three witnesses who have actually seen the transgression. Then, and only then, if the brother or sister continues to refuse to see it and repent, take it to the fellowship as a whole for exposure.

Never should it be passed mouth to mouth and ear to ear in the shadows. Never does the very necessary process of correction begin with talking it around. Never should this be done before there's been a one-on-one confrontation in private with love and respect. Shem and Japheth covered their father's failure, his shame, and nakedness, and backed up to him with a garment covering them so that they themselves would not see it. Love *covers* a multitude of sins. Honor respects a brother or sister even in failure, and the result is authority, inheritance, blessing, and prosperity.

> So, as those who have been chosen of God, holy and beloved, put on a heart of compassion, kindness, humility, gentleness and patience; bearing with one another, and forgiving each other, whoever has a complaint against anyone; just as the Lord forgave you, so also should you. Beyond all these things put on love, which is the perfect bond of unity.
>
> (Colossians 3:12–14)

HONORING LEADERS

Finally, there is Hebrews 13:17–18:

> Obey your leaders and submit to them, for they keep watch over your souls as those who will give an account. Let them do this with joy and not with grief, for this would be unprofitable for you. Pray for us, for we are sure that we have a good conscience, desiring to conduct ourselves honorably in all things.

Hebrews 13 speaks to several components of a culture of love and honor. As we have been called to honor one another as brothers and sisters, the Scripture commands us to honor those who lead. God will hold those of us who lead accountable for the manner in which we lead and for how well we keep watch over the well-being of those given into our care. This makes for a heavy burden, especially when honor goes missing. Most who enter full-time ministry in our day will not finish in ministry. Research I read somewhere says that only one in five of those who graduate from a seminary or Bible college will still be in ministry five years later.

As I travel to minister in various places internationally, I meet more people who once served in ministry than I do those currently in ministry. The burden of leadership can tear you apart at the core of your identity. The stress of it often ruins families and erodes physical health. I once heard the late Jack Frost say that only one in forty who enter pastoral ministry will still be in ministry at the time of retirement. The burden of it destroys and burns them out.

> HONORING OUR LEADERS MEANS GIVING THEM THE GRACE TO BE IMPERFECT, TO FAIL, TO SAY THE WRONG THINGS, AND TO GET IT WRONG FROM TIME TO TIME.

The author of Hebrews exhorted the people of God to let those in authority lead with joy, to honor them in such a way as to lift the burden and allow them to see the fruit of their labor. This means giving them the grace to be imperfect, to fail, to say the wrong things in the wrong ways, and to get it wrong from time to time. They need the freedom to be as human as anyone else.

THE PROMISE

A promise comes with all of this. In a culture of honor, when a people honor their leaders and cover their failings in the way that love covers a multitude of sins, the people of God prosper. A people will destroy themselves who fail to honor their leadership and who allow themselves to fall into criticism and exposure of the nakedness of their spiritual leaders. They'll cut off their own blessing and, in many cases, they'll actually blame the leader for their loss.

At this writing, I have forty years' experience traveling all over the United States and in foreign nations as a speaker and prophetic voice. A distressing number of the churches I have ministered in over the years no longer exist, and in nearly every case that I have been able to track, a culture of love and honor was lacking, either for each other or for their leadership.

What makes places like Bethel Church in Redding, California, fly and become major forces internationally is not that they have a focus on the supernatural (for which they are well-known) or the Lord's power. It's that they cultivate a culture of love and honor. Even in the face of failure, error, and missteps they hold that course. With a consistent determination to honor leadership comes the promise of profit to the people of God. No leader can be fully effective for the benefit of the people in the face of dishonor and unbelief.

> WITH A CONSISTENT DETERMINATION TO HONOR LEADERSHIP COMES THE PROMISE OF PROFIT TO THE PEOPLE OF GOD.

We're playing watermelon football in this culture of love and honor. It's a fragile thing, easily damaged and broken. It needs diligent care and nurture to be passed from one to another with faithfulness and sensitivity. Please understand that these issues of honor I'm stressing have everything to do with holiness. God will judge failures of honor in the same way that He will judge other issues of sin and compromise.

WE'RE NOT ON OUR OWN

The good news is that we're not on our own. We have a heavenly coach, a powerful Counselor who dwells within us and who has written His Word for us to study and learn from. We need only listen and then act on what we read and hear, allowing Him to honor and love through us. I've learned the hard way that if I rely on my own fleshly ability to love and honor, I'll fail, as I've done so many times over all my years of full-time ministry since 1976. Jesus told us that apart from Him, we can do nothing, and I am living proof.

In John 14:12, Jesus promised that we would do greater works than He did. I wonder if we've equated that promise only with signs, wonders, healings, and deliverance? I believe that would be a mistake. His love, and the gift of honor it brings, are also the works of Jesus that come with the promise. This explains why the apostle Paul in 1 Corinthians 13 first mentioned gifts of the Spirit, then listed faith, hope, and love as the things that last, and finished by saying that the greatest of these is love. If love does not include the gift of honor, it cannot be love. Where honor and love go, miracles and manifestations of God's presence follow.

> A CULTURE OF LOVE AND HONOR RELEASES AN ATMOSPHERE
> IN WHICH MIRACLES CAN HAPPEN BECAUSE
> IT REFLECTS THE NATURE OF JESUS.

Signs and wonders do little or nothing to create a culture of honor. It's actually the other way around. Lack of honor hinders signs and wonders. Because of a lack of honor, not even Jesus could do many miracles in His hometown. (See Matthew 13:57–58.) A culture of love and honor releases an atmosphere in which miracles can happen because it reflects the nature of Jesus. Where the kind of love and honor I'm talking about does not exist, power is hindered and miracles dry up. I would suspect that when miracles aren't happening on a regular basis, the problem *might* be lack of faith, but even more likely is the absence of real love and genuine honor.

I'm speaking of the kind of love and honor that covers a multitude of sins, the kind that forgives seventy times seven, the kind that doesn't measure failures, and the kind that redeems the weaknesses of men like John Mark who abandoned Barnabas and Saul on their first missionary journey. This kind of honor can seem to be difficult, but we have been promised a Counselor to help us.

Many influential people wrote off my brother Mark as a leader many years ago, but he spent eleven years as the spiritual director of a major international ministry and a year and a half as its president. Now he successfully leads a new international ministry called Elijah Rain Ministries. All of this came about through the power of a culture of honor and love. Good people, empowered by the Holy Spirit, believed in him when others would not. With honor came the promise of blessing and profit to the body of Christ.

We have a man in our church whom I'll call Tom. He knows he's a few French fries short of a Happy Meal and we lovingly tease him about that. It's part of the glory and gifting God has placed in Him. He knows there have been relationships he's had to repair and times he's needed to apologize for his insensitivity, just like any of the rest of us, but he's probably the boldest, most effective evangelist we have. I believe in him, and if he has shortcomings and failings, I'll cover that nakedness and honor what God has put in him.

From a fleshly perspective, we're playing watermelon football, but we have the promise of a coach who gets us to the goal line if we will but listen and refuse to rely on our own resources to get there. Scripture says the flesh avails nothing. If it's not His love flowing through me, my love hurts people. If He's not with me and I'm not in Him, I'm a failure. If it's not His power in me and through me, then it all comes out wrong. It's the Spirit of the Living God, our Counselor, our Advocate, our Teacher, who shows us how to play the game.

WE MUST BE KNOWN FOR LOVE

On one side of a culture of honor, we see all the things we say to one another to uplift and encourage. It's the attitude of the heart that believes the unbelievable in one another. It's seeing the glory of the image of God implanted into each of us and affirming it with our words and actions. It's encouragement, exhortation, and strengthening.

On the other side, it's forgiveness and forbearance. It's covering the nakedness of our brothers, sisters, and leaders. It's love covering every failure and every wrong word. It's the surrender of every offense. It's giving one another the space to fail, to be wrong. It's grace for hurts, wounds, and inner brokenness. It's refusing to participate in gangrenous talk that spreads death and negativity.

It's praising and worshiping God with passion and love while never allowing human failure to get in the way. The Lord's church must be known for its love. Can we come before the throne of God and surrender anything that forms a barrier to that? Can we make a covenant commitment to love and honor until it becomes a culture that conditions every one of us in the Holy Spirit to think, move, and act in love and honor?

9

STORMS OF CHANGE

As early as 2009, the Lord began warning me of approaching storms that would radically change the world as we have known it. These are strong winds blowing with tornado strength and force to dramatically impact both civilization and the body of Christ.

FIVE WHITE TORNADOES

In April 2009, I had a dream in which five white tornadoes were coming toward me across an open field lined with buildings on either side perhaps a hundred yards apart. The sun stood at my back and lit the approaching tornadoes in white light. None of this frightened me. I was actually filled with an inexplicable sense of excitement. Some of my church people had gathered behind me and I turned to reassure them that this was a good thing.

In May 2010, I attended a conference at what was then the Toronto Airport Christian Fellowship. Just before I boarded the flight from Denver to Toronto, my brother Mark handed me a stack of frightening doom-and-gloom prophecies that he wanted me to evaluate, coming from a long list of people both in and out of the body of Christ. At the conference, as I pondered these prophecies in the midst of a powerful time of worship, the Lord said, "You have five years in which to prepare."

Immediately, I thought of five as the symbolic number for grace and anticipated an indeterminate period of God's grace before the coming crisis would come to pass. But then, much later, the coronavirus crisis began to unfold and I was prompted to review old dream journals and put some dates together. As I did this, the five years suddenly became much more literal as you are about to see.

> THE LORD SAID, "YOU HAVE FOUR YEARS IN WHICH TO PREPARE.
> YOU HAVE LOST THE ART OF THE TREMBLE."

As previously referenced, on December 5, 2016, during a prayer meeting at my church, I received a vision of four sticks standing up with the fourth one bending. The Lord said, "You have four years in which to prepare. You have lost the art of the tremble." I understood that there would be some kind of downturn in the president's fourth year and that, for the sake of preparation, it was important that we recover the fear of the Lord. Then came the Russian collusion investigation, the attempt to impeach the president, and, finally, the coronavirus crisis with its economic consequences.

In a dream on January 22, 2016, I saw a woman with a clear angelic air about her leading me from a small boat up onto a lonely muddy land that was void of vegetation. I knew she was taking me to an important meeting of some kind. As we walked, she very mysteriously informed me, "There are going to be two more." I understood her to mean that two more would be coming to the meeting.

The meeting itself turned out to be a kind of banquet with the president of the United States. It seemed as though we were late to arrive because everyone had left except the president. He received me graciously and invited me to take some food. Not much was left, but it was enough, although it was cold because the banquet had ended and no one remained but the president himself.

I then sensed that the next president was about to arrive. At the same time, on what appeared to be a stage a few steps up from me, I saw another dinner, a fresh feast laid out and prepared. As I moved to investigate the food, I sensed that the new president was almost there, as if just outside. I had a very good feeling about this next president.

ADDED UP, WHAT DOES IT MEAN?

I had the five tornadoes dream in 2009. Tornadoes symbolically represent sudden cataclysmic change. Then in May 2010, God spoke the word about five years in which to prepare. That led to May 2015. Donald Trump openly declared his candidacy on June 16, 2015, five years and less than one month later. Thus began the first of the five tornadoes bringing radical and dramatic change with Trump as both wrecking ball and master rebuilder. In October 2016, just before the election, I heard God say, "Trump will win, but he will not serve." In other words, he would not serve the system as it was. He certainly has not.

The second tornado corresponds to the failed Russian collusion investigation that tore the country apart in the midst of a roaring economy or *feast* as in the January 2016 dream.

Tornado number three took shape as the failed drive to impeach the president further divided the nation in the midst of what remained an economic feast.

> THE COVID-19 CRISIS THAT WRECKED THE ECONOMY AND THREW THE NATION INTO UNPRECEDENTED CHAOS MADE THE FOURTH OF THE FIVE TORNADOES.

The Covid-19 crisis that wrecked the economy and threw the nation into unprecedented chaos made the fourth of the five tornadoes, bringing dramatic and even catastrophic change. The feast that had been the economic abundance from my dream of January 22, 2016, then grew cold with little remaining on the table, just as in the dream. Each successive tornado has been more intense than the one that came before it.

Yet to come is the fifth tornado. At this point, it's important to remember that these are *white tornadoes*, indicating that God is using them bring about His purposes. As I write these words in May 2020, I see that one of the purposes of the fourth tornado has been to humble and refine Donald Trump in order to break away the outer crust of his rough persona to reveal the gentle and compassionate man God has made him to be. If we will pray for him with honor and respect, especially as the new Christian he is, then fresh light from the Holy Spirit will flow through him to expose and shame the wickedness of those who have been his enemies.

In the banquet room in the January 2016 dream, a new feast was laid out and prepared for the arrival of the new president. I believe prosperity, a fresh feast, will be restored before Trump leaves office. It will be on the table and ready for the next president to preside over.

More importantly, I believe the season of the fifth tornado will include one of the most dramatic and powerful revivals in history. More than just an economic feast, it will be a season of feasting in the Holy Spirit. The first four tornadoes have set the stage for this by shaking everything that can be shaken. The remnant have taken the shaking to heart in repentance and purification, especially during the fourth tornado Covid-19 crisis.

The angel began the dream in January 2016 by saying, "There are going to be two more." I suspect that we will see a second version of Donald Trump, humbled, shaken, and shaped by the Covid-19 crisis. We will see a Donald Trump, version two, presiding over the second and higher feast.

> WE OF THE REMNANT HAVE BEEN CALLED TO INTENSE PRAYER ROOTED IN REPENTANCE FOR OUR NATIONAL SINS AND FOR THOSE OF THE BODY OF CHRIST.

Whatever all of this may mean, we of the remnant have been called to intense prayer rooted in repentance for our national sins and for those of the body of Christ. In this way, we lay the groundwork for revival and we begin to recover our lost authority to speak into this culture.

The wind of the Spirit in the fifth tornado will radically change the heart and spirit of the church in an outpouring unlike anything we've seen in our lifetime. Meanwhile, the simultaneous storm wind of societal decay and destruction will continue to rock the world and devastate nations.

PROPHECIES NOW UNFOLDING

In December 2014, the Lord told me we would see such levels of corruption exposed in the United States government that it would shock the nation. I included this in my annual prophetic word for 2015. As I write, the covers are being torn off of such widespread and deep corruption as has not been seen in my lifetime. The legislative branch of the United States government seems paralyzed to get anything done in the face of what has surfaced or been alleged on both sides of the political aisle. I have seen the same in Canada and in Europe as governments seem unable or unwilling to deal effectively with any of the emerging issues. Economies, cultures, and senses of national identity are under assault. The storm is brewing…and it has only just begun.

THIS IS WAR

For our struggle is not against flesh and blood, but against the rulers, against the powers, against the world forces of this darkness, against the spiritual forces of wickedness in the heavenly places. (Ephesians 6:12)

We contend against high-level demonic forces ruling over regions and cultures. The Greek word for these ruling spirits indicates overarching powers exerting dominant influence. The passage goes on to speak of *schema* in the Greek, which literally means "schemes" or "well-laid plans."

DEMONIC PRINCIPALITIES SHAPE THE CULTURE AND THOUGHT OF ENTIRE SOCIETIES. THOSE WHO DISAGREE ARE THEN SEEN AS IGNORANT, THE ENEMY, A THREAT, AND DANGEROUS.

Demonic principalities shape the culture and thought of entire societies until their diabolical ways of thinking, the evil they promote, comes to seem good and self-evident to the majority of those in the cultures they influence. Those who disagree are then seen as ignorant, the enemy, a threat, and dangerous. Sound familiar?

THE SPIRIT OF BAAL

In ancient Israel, Baal was the dominant principality. Subtly, over time, Baal infiltrated Israel's culture and faith, gradually conditioning the people to accept the worship of idols with all of the accompanying hideous practices. Just like some 75 percent of the population today claims to be Christian while holding an antichrist worldview, the people of Israel didn't see themselves as rejecting Yahweh, at least at first.

As the influence of Baal insinuated itself into their lives, passages like Isaiah 58 reveal that the people began to adopt self-serving ways in addition to foreign concepts, immorality, and polluted worship with which the Lord confronted them in previous chapters of Isaiah. They refused to believe that they had compromised anything concerning the Lord, but as they cried out to Him, fasting and praying, desiring to know why God didn't hear their prayers, the Lord took note of their complaint and responded in Isaiah 58:3–4:

> *"Why have we fasted and You do not see? Why have we humbled ourselves and You do not notice?" Behold, on the day of your fast you find your desire, and drive hard all your workers. Behold, you fast for contention and strife and to strike with a wicked fist. You do not fast like you do today to make your voice heard on high.*

Eventually the influence of the spirit of Baal became so dominant that when true prophets—always the minority—challenged the demonic way of thinking that affected their culture and their worship, Israel responded by persecuting, imprisoning, and killing them. Today, we who stand for righteousness and holiness find ourselves labeled as bigots and hate-mongers. Demonic cultural conditioning has been changing the face of Christianity itself in grotesque and destructive ways. The coming outpouring of glory in the Holy Spirit therefore belongs to those numbered among the one hundred and forty-four thousand faithful I spoke of earlier. The remnant rises!

FOUR MARKS OF THE DOMINANCE OF THE SPIRIT OF BAAL

The same demon—literally—that seduced and ultimately destroyed Israel now pervasively infects and influences the culture of the western world and has even invaded much of the church, warping her doctrines and leading to acceptance of what the Bible calls sin. Baal, the same demonic principality that dominated the culture of ancient Israel, now dominates the thought and practice of our modern culture.

> BAAL, THE SAME DEMONIC PRINCIPALITY THAT DOMINATED THE CULTURE OF ANCIENT ISRAEL, NOW DOMINATES THE THOUGHT AND PRACTICE OF OUR MODERN CULTURE.

Scripture records four marks of the dominance of the Baal spirit as it infected Israel. I'll summarize them quickly because the good news overshadows the bad.

CONSUMING SELF-FOCUS

At its heart, Baalism was a fertility cult focused on prosperity. As a goal, prosperity expresses and feeds a consuming focus on self, while it leads us to offer certain sacrifices to ensure that self is served.

We baby boomers, born in the years following World War II, became known as the *me generation*. Because of us, self-focus has become the dominant force driving the cultural soup in which we live. Focus on self has infected and eventually stifled every move of the Holy Spirit in my lifetime as it has shaped doctrines, ministries, and worship styles. Christian counseling became less about the cross, repentance, and holiness, and more about being *happy*. Doctrines became less and less about the sacrifice of the cross and more about health, wealth, and supernatural experiences. Worship morphed from being about loving and blessing God to being an entertainment event designed to draw and please the masses.

The selflessness and sacrifice of the cross—becoming like Jesus—has too often been supplanted by, "Jesus died to make me rich, so tell me what buttons to push or words to confess to make that happen," or, "Jesus died to take away my pain." For too many, the cry of the heart is, "Heal me, bless me, love me... but don't challenge me."

But Jesus didn't die to make us rich or happy. He died to make us holy, that we might be conformed to the image of the Son.

RAMPANT SEXUAL IMMORALITY

In Israel's day, Baal worship included the use of temple prostitutes as a kind of sympathetic magic to ensure the growth of crops and the multiplication of livestock. If you wanted to release fertility on your flocks and crops, you had sex with a temple prostitute called a *priestess*. In certain cases, the practice even included homosexual male temple prostitutes.

> *There were also male cult prostitutes in the land. They did according to all the abominations of the nations which the* Lord *dispossessed before the sons of Israel.*
>
> (1 Kings 14:24)

From there, sexual immorality and perversion infected the culture as a whole and came to be the accepted cultural norm.

He also broke down the houses of the male cult prostitutes which were in the house of the LORD, *where the women were weaving hangings for the Asherah.*　　(2 Kings 23:7)

I will not punish your daughters when they play the harlot or your brides when they commit adultery, for the men themselves go apart with harlots and offer sacrifices with temple prostitutes; so the people without understanding are ruined.　　(Hosea 4:14)

In today's culture, even those who claim to honor the authority of Scripture treat sexual immorality as a normal thing, something to be expected when an unmarried couple "love" one another. In a single generation, we've gone from married TV couples sleeping in separate beds—in *I Love Lucy, Leave It to Beaver, The Dick Van Dyke Show,* and other series—to complete sex acts on screen between couples, married or not, both heterosexual and homosexual. Media present this as normal and good, the natural and immediate result of two people liking each other, complete with romantic music playing in the background. Even our comic book superheroes in the movies, presented as icons of what is good and right, cross the moral line sexually. Superman sleeps with his girlfriend. So does Thor. Whether it's sci-fi or fantasy, drama or comedy, nearly every television series or movie today includes a gay couple, presented as normal, acceptable, and desirable.

The church has contributed to this by failing to teach God's vision of the glory of sexual union in marriage, choosing too often instead to adopt a view of sexuality as fleshly and shameful on the one hand, or giving permission on the other hand for unmarried people to sin sexually under the covering of easy grace. This has rendered us vulnerable to a demonic way of thinking that says sex is good, but promotes it outside the boundaries prescribed by God to preserve its glory and goodness. The result has been an exponential increase in pornography and perversion, often defended as normal and blessed by God.

SACRIFICE OF THE CHILDREN

"For the sons of Judah have done that which is evil in My sight," declares the LORD, "they have set their detestable things in the house which is called by My name, to defile it. They have built the high places of Topheth, which is in the valley of the son of Hinnom, to burn their sons and their daughters in the fire, which I did not command, and it did not come into My mind." (Jeremiah 7:30–31)

IN MODERN TIMES, WE SEE A HOLOCAUST OF TENS OF MILLIONS OF UNBORN CHILDREN SACRIFICED ON THE ALTAR OF OUR CULTURAL SELF-ABSORPTION, THE ALTAR OF BAAL.

In modern times, we see a holocaust of tens of millions of unborn children sacrificed on the altar of our cultural self-absorption, the altar of Baal, and we call it a woman's right. When a culture as a whole speaks of evil as good and good as evil, demonic domination is at work at the level of a principality.

CUTTING AND SELF-MUTILATION

In 1 Kings 18, Elijah challenged the prophets of Baal to a contest. Whose God would send fire from heaven? He stood alone against four-hundred and fifty of the opposition. Notice what the prophets of Baal did as they sought to summon power:

"So they cried with a loud voice and cut themselves according to their custom with swords and lances until the blood gushed out on them" (1 Kings 18:28).

I have been told by reliable youth leaders that one in three teens cuts. They do it as an outlet for a depth of emotional pain they can express in no other way, to get power over that pain when they feel powerless. Our self-absorbed generation has effectively abandoned them. They live in an uncertain world without boundaries or guidelines, with no one but peers to whom to pour out emotions they can't possibly understand, full of fear and loss of hope. Unwittingly, they cut as a blood sacrifice to Baal, who promises power over powerlessness.

Cutting to gain power can be no coincidence. I see the evidence and influence of the Baal spirit behind it. Baal delights in the murder of unborn children and the mutilation of the young, as well as the shedding of blood for the sake of promises he will not and cannot keep.

THE COMING STORM OF WOE

When a demonic principality rules a culture and has so infected its thinking that evil appears to be self-evidently good and good appears to be self-evidently evil, and when those who stand for the good become the enemy and are labeled in negative ways, then historically, in virtually every case, the only remedy left for God has been to apply catastrophic national or cultural calamity. Repentance would turn the tide, but it seldom happens once the culture has set its course.

> THE ONLY REMEDY LEFT FOR GOD IS TO APPLY CATASTROPHIC NATIONAL OR CULTURAL CALAMITY.

I did not want to see what the Lord showed me concerning this. I wanted to accept the idea of a great culture-sweeping, culture-changing revival, an America and western world restored and redeemed. The culture as a whole, however, has made a firm and settled decision concerning a number of moral issues. That decision will not be unmade. This, however, is not the last word. Please bear with me because good news is coming.

In Bible times, genuine prophets and those who stood for righteousness were labeled as enemies. Prophets who spoke the truth were sidelined and imprisoned. They threw Jeremiah down a well. Micaiah found himself imprisoned and fed meager rations of bread and water. Both men were lonely voices crying out warnings in a sea of other so-called prophets who spoke only positive messages in the face of Israel's growing apostasy.

As Israel resisted the words of God's true prophets, He sent judgment before He sent wrath. As opposed to punishment or vengeance, judgment is pressure sent to separate the precious from the vile and thereby spark repentance. When judgment fails to inspire repentance, then comes wrath, the last resort of a loving God seeking to break the stronghold of destructive demonic thinking.

In 722 BC, Assyria destroyed the northern kingdom of Israel when the nation refused to listen to plumb-line prophets like Elijah whom God sent to warn them. That kingdom never came back. For the sake of God's promise to David, the southern kingdom, Judah, and its capital, Jerusalem, stumbled on until 586 BC, when absolute destruction came at the hands of Babylon. The cream of the nation was then carried into seventy years of exile.

The Babylonian captivity cured Israel of the Baal infection and broke the hold of that demonic principality on the minds and hearts of the people. It took that catastrophic national calamity, however, to free them of the evil mentality and restore them to the law of God and morality.

In the United States, the principality driving racism made slavery and the idea that Africans were inferior seem self-evident, the natural order of things, twisting the clear teaching of the Scriptures to support it. So deeply rooted was this way of thinking that even many of those who saw slavery as cruel and wrong held on to the lie that Africans were lesser human beings. In the eyes of those caught up in the dominance of that principality, any who stood for truth and righteousness became the enemy, attacked and ridiculed.

Once this demonic influence had been so firmly established in the culture—good seen as evil and evil seen as good—and when the pressure of judgment failed, the only way it could begin to be dislodged was by a catastrophic national calamity that would shatter the structure of the culture that spawned it. Our nation therefore suffered the Civil War, the most bloody and destructive in our history. It was fought at first under the banner of states' rights and the quest to preserve the union. Only later did it come to be framed as the war to free the slaves.

In the 1930s, Germany descended into anti-Semitism under Hitler's fascist regime. People like Dietrich Bonhoeffer and the German Confessing Church tried to speak into that gathering darkness and turn the tide against the Nazis, but the nation didn't listen. The demonic principality fueling anti-Semitism twisted the thinking of an entire nation until the dominant culture saw white Aryans as the master race and Jews as *untermenschen* (subhumans) who were self-evidently evil, the cause of all the world's troubles, and therefore worthy of extermination. Bonhoeffer and others who functioned as the prophets of righteousness ended up in concentration camps.

It took a catastrophic national calamity—the defeat and utter crushing of Germany, the loss of an entire generation of young men, and the dividing of the nation—to break the hold of that demonic principality over the minds and hearts of the German people. The culture had to be broken.

Now we have North America—and by extension, the rest of the world—influenced by our culture and entertainment industry dominated by the Baal spirit.

Culture-wide, good is regarded as evil and evil is regarded as good; those who stand for righteousness are labeled as hateful bigots, enemies of the social order.

> **WE HAVE PASSED THE POINT OF BEING CAPABLE OF SUFFICIENT NATIONAL OR SOCIETAL REPENTANCE.**

I fear that we have passed the point of being capable of sufficient national or societal repentance. A cultural decision has been made and the course has been set, although we do see windows of seeming respite from the trend. God is being written out of national life, although under the current president, we may enjoy somewhat of a reprieve from pressure, a renewed *feast*, until he is out of office. In the church, the gospel is too often watered down, worship becomes a truncated entertainment event, and morality is compromised. We've lost our voice in the culture as a result.

I fear that, like every empire that has gone before us, only a catastrophic destruction can serve to break the hold of the demonic influence on our culture and restore us to our true selves. Repentance could change things, and I pray that it comes, but for there to be repentance, there must be a sense of sin. Individuals and cultures in need of repentance must have a consciousness of what has been lost that must be reclaimed.

THE LOSS OF CULTURAL AGREEMENT

In the days leading up to the first and second Great Awakenings on the East Coast of North America, for instance, the culture of the time, although fallen into sin, still held an agreed-upon sense of right and wrong. Calls for repentance made sense to people because everyone in the 1700s and 1800s understood the baseline. They knew what they had departed from and could therefore respond to a call to return.

Today, for the first time in the history of the western world—and North America in particular—we no longer enjoy a cultural agreement concerning basic issues of morality. The moral plumb line has vanished. Anything goes. No longer is there an effective consciousness of sin. Even in much of the church, *sin* is a word seldom heard. If there is no sin, repentance becomes an empty concept. The culture has denied the Lord, invalidated His laws, and passed apostasy into law. Morality is now defined as relative to the individual. The Word of God has become irrelevant and moral absolutes are hard to find.

Hello, Baal.

Sin kills. Lives are destroyed. Babies are murdered in the womb, and now even at the point of birth. Families break up. Crime rates rise and prison populations swell. Hatred proliferates and washes over the societal landscape like a tidal wave, sweeping everything in its path. A truly loving God *must* act to stem the tide and end the pain. I fear that catastrophic destruction may finally be the only recourse left to our God to remedy the situation for our own sake.

> CATASTROPHIC DESTRUCTION MAY FINALLY BE THE ONLY RECOURSE LEFT TO OUR GOD TO REMEDY THE SITUATION FOR OUR OWN SAKE.

"The angel of the LORD *encamps around those who fear Him, and rescues them"* (Psalm 34:7). In the absence of true fear of God among the nations of the western world, the angel of the Lord no longer encamps around us. Consequently, a crisis approaches and there are no truly great men waiting in the wings to lead us as in every other crisis the nations of the free world have faced.

In the United States, we had George Washington to shepherd us through the crisis of the Revolutionary War. Even during the trauma of the Civil War in the U.S., there remained a cultural agreement about morality. Both sides acknowledged God at every level, even in their error and sin. God therefore gave the nation Abraham Lincoln, a great man to lead us through the crisis. During the Great Depression and into World War II, we had Franklin D. Roosevelt. British Prime Minister Winston Churchill rose to greatness, along with military leaders such as Field Marshall Bernard Law Montgomery, General George S. Patton, and others. God gave us a Ronald Reagan to lead the free world to victory in the Cold War.

Today, unfortunately, no great men wait in the wings to lead us out of the crisis to come. The angel of Lord no longer encamps around us. For all the controversy he generates, Donald Trump carries the gifts to buy us some time, perhaps years, but he does not rise to the level of greatness needed to weather the storm that will inevitably come. God can turn the worst sinner into a great man or woman, but it will require prayer, honor, and love of the highest order to bring that about. Turmoil, collapse and, yes, war lie before us, and we believers must prepare.

THE COMING STORM OF GLORY

In the face of what is to come, we must deeply root ourselves in the truth that Jesus alone is King. Jesus alone is our government. Our citizenship rests in the kingdom of God that transcends all nationalities, races, and ethnicities. We are citizens of the kingdom of God before all other loyalties. Jesus alone is our hope, our provider, our security, and our glory.

The storm—the tornado—of the Holy Spirit is about to break upon us. For the church, the faithful, our greatest glory unfolds in the midst of this difficult time. Greatness lies ahead for us. In the midst of it all, we get to win in ways we have never seen before.

In the mystery of prophetic perspective, Isaiah said it best when he prophesied both Israel's return from exile and the glory to come upon a generation of believers who would live in a time that remained for him far distant.

> *Arise, shine; for your light has come, and the glory of the* LORD *has risen upon you. For behold, darkness will cover the earth and deep darkness the peoples; but the* LORD *will rise upon you and His glory will appear upon you. Nations will come to your light, and kings to the brightness of your rising.* (Isaiah 60:1–3)

Deep darkness is coming to the world around us and has already begun to unfold. This cannot be avoided now. If we who are called by the Lord's name will change our harsh and judgmental tone and go deeply into the Father's love and the Father's heart, and if we will radiate grace and love from the Holy Spirit within us to this world, proving and demonstrating what God is really like, then in the midst of the whirlwind, we will bring in the greatest harvest of souls the world has ever seen. We will walk in the greatest sense of the presence of the Lord we've ever known, and signs and wonders will be the order of the day. We stand now at the threshold of our greatest glory and joy.

IF WE WHO ARE CALLED BY THE LORD'S NAME WILL RADIATE GRACE AND LOVE FROM THE HOLY SPIRIT WITHIN US, WE WILL BRING IN THE GREATEST HARVEST OF SOULS THE WORLD HAS EVER SEEN.

Isaiah continued, *"Lift up your eyes round about and see; they all gather together, they come to you. Your sons will come from afar, and your daughters will be carried in the arms"* (Isaiah 60:4). While the darkness gathers, the world will come to us for the answers it needs, drawn by the light emanating from us.

None of these promises happened in fullness for literal Israel, but God promises these things to those who follow Jesus.

Then you will see and be radiant, and your heart will thrill and rejoice; because the abundance of the sea will be turned to you, the wealth of the nations will come to you.

(Isaiah 60:5)

Later in the same chapter:

No longer will you have the sun for light by day, nor for brightness will the moon give you light; but you will have the LORD for an everlasting light, and your God for your glory. Your sun will no longer set, nor will your moon wane; for you will have the LORD for an everlasting light, and the days of your mourning will be over. Then all your people will be righteous; they will possess the land forever, the branch of My planting, the work of My hands, that I may be glorified. The smallest one will become a clan, and the least one a mighty nation. I, the LORD, will hasten it in its time.

(Isaiah 60:19–22)

Isaiah saw a distant promise for a time yet to come. Only in Jesus could all the people of God be made righteous. He cleansed us and made us holy by His sacrifice for sin on the cross. In Him, the fullness of Isaiah's word is fulfilled as the number of God's people has grown to such an extent that it cannot even be accurately measured.

These promises were never truly realized in the history of literal Israel, but they are fulfilled in Jesus and they will be fully realized among us in these last days. In the midst of world crises and troubles, the time of the fulfillment of Isaiah's prophecy lies before us. It applies to those who have prepared themselves in purity, integrity, and unpolluted devotion to Jesus.

Lighthouse ministries, communities of refuge, are even now emerging in cities all around the world. As people begin to figure out that sin doesn't work, and as suffering mounts in the midst of war and economic and societal collapse, they'll be looking for places where the love, mercy, grace, and power of our Savior manifest. God is and will be igniting bonfires of revival, strategically placed and made visible to the world around them, so people will know where to find hope and healing.

> GOD IS AND WILL BE IGNITING BONFIRES OF REVIVAL, STRATEGICALLY PLACED AND MADE VISIBLE TO THE WORLD, SO PEOPLE WILL KNOW WHERE TO FIND HOPE AND HEALING.

GOD'S COMING *REDO* IN FOUR MAJOR ISSUES

Will there be revival? Absolutely. It will be the most powerful since Pentecost. Even now, it begins with four major *reissues*.

1. RE*DEPLOYMENT*

Under an administration that favors the church and Israel, we have lived in a season of grace and ease, but saw that disrupted under the impact of the Covid-19 crisis. In the face of such trial and turmoil, certain models of watered-down church life and faith turn out to be insufficient to sustain people. As time passes, God will be *redeploying* His people to ministries where depths of worship, meaty teaching, and effective pastoral care for helping and healing are available to impart the strengths needed for perseverance in love, power, and joy.

Where doctrinal drift has happened and foundational truths have been compromised, and where sin in leadership has been exposed, increasing numbers of people will find themselves shaken by the resulting instability. Again, I say that we will see a population shift in the church, not to places where doctrine has become an idol, or where the religious spirit has suppressed or destroyed the spirit of love and freedom, but to places of firm foundation in the eternal revelation of who God is and what He calls us to be.

2. REFORMATION

Church leaders, from pastors to prophets, apostles to lay leaders, will be—and are being—reshaped and remolded to conform to the image of the Son for the building up and *reforming* of the body of Christ. God will be diminishing the profiles of those who have built ministries around exaltation of their own names and ambitions. Cults of personality, as well as ministries built on forms of domination and control, will be reduced and in some cases dismantled, as the hand of the Lord brings humility and the true heart of the Father's love to His anointed ones. For some in leadership, this will mean being installed in different or altered positions, which points back to *redeployment*. This may create confusion in some as they question where God is taking them.

Prophetic ministry will undergo a radical purge, a purifying and a cleansing. Among some, this is already underway. Where we have practiced an unbalanced emphasis on personal prophecy, true prophetic voices will increasingly emerge to separate the precious from the vile, calling for repentance and holiness in the tradition of the prophets of old. Where prediction is part of this, the purpose will be preparation of the body of Christ for things to come. We will therefore see a blending of the functions of the Old Testament prophets as they confronted Israel's sin, compromise and apostasy, with those of New Testament prophets like Agabus in giving encouragement, releasing promise, and preparing the church for what lies ahead.

Changes will come about in the way church is done, if not in outward form, then in orientation of the heart. Forms of church government are not the issue, as many have asserted. A wise seminary professor once said to me, "No structure of church government is any better than the people involved." These changes have more to do with issues of the heart that will affect the way ministries relate to people, no matter how those ministries are organizationally structured. Outward forms of church life may not change, but the substance that fills them will.

Church leadership worthy of receiving the redeployed saints will be moving into a deeper understanding of what God has truly designed their roles to be in releasing a kingdom culture of honor and love, equipping the saints and freeing them to realize the dreams and purposes God has placed in their hearts.

3. REPENTANCE

Increasingly, across a broad range of ministries, God will be exposing that which fails to reflect the nature of Jesus and does not spring from a hunger for holiness in His image. This has been true in national and international leadership for some time now, but conviction is yet to come in fullness upon the wider people of God. Increasingly, He will be turning willing hearts away from living life according to the flesh and toward life lived by the Holy Spirit, who puts to death the deeds of the flesh and brings real life.

4. RELEASE

Freedom is coming for God's people to walk in their gifts without the pressure of domination or control, freed from leadership that feels threatened when the saints walk freely in the fullness of their anointings. We in leadership must carry the heart of the Father for His people. Every real father wants his children to do better and more than he did. Jesus said in John 14:12 that because He was going to the Father, we who believe would do even greater works than He did in His earthly walk. In that spirit, we in leadership must lift our people higher in the gifts God has given them than we ourselves have risen.

This does not mean there will be no leadership. Those who advocate a leaderless church have neither heard accurately from God, nor have they read the Scripture in context. It means, rather, that church leadership will increasingly come to understand the meaning of their task. The saints will walk in freedom, even while respecting the authority and guidance of those God has placed in authority. So, I call upon believers to renew their hope where hope has faltered. Jesus remains Lord and He will accomplish His purposes through those who are willing.

BIRTH PANGS

Meanwhile, the earth begins to groan in labor with the birth pangs of the coming of the kingdom of God, as it can no longer bear up under the burden of the accumulated sin of mankind. Natural disasters, diseases, and human suffering will multiply. Economies will collapse. Already, we have seen this in the coronavirus crisis. On the one hand, this can be regarded as a huge negative. On the other hand, every birth involves pain and stretching of the body, followed by a period of recovery. In the end, the pain of labor brings a wonderful new life into the world. The kingdom of God is coming and all creation travails to give birth.

> ## THE KINGDOM OF GOD IS COMING AND ALL CREATION TRAVAILS TO GIVE BIRTH.

According to Matthew 24, these things must unfold, but they are not the final word. Jesus actually told us that we must not be afraid when we see these things. A major element of our calling is to be present in love for people in the midst of it all, ready to heal hurts and minister to those lost in the unfolding turmoil.

If you are in a church or ministry determined to be a lighthouse in the sense I've described, you've probably faced a lot of trouble as the enemy of our soul has instigated opposition and created trials. Nothing has been easy. It has, however, been a time of refining that leads to the realization of God's purposes.

And we know that God causes all things to work together for good to those who love God, to those who are called according to His purpose. For those whom He foreknew, He also predestined to become conformed to the image of His Son.   (Romans 8:28–29)

The good that all of the hardship and heartache produces by the hand of God is transformation into representations of what Jesus is really like.

The verses leading to Roman 8:28–29 speak directly to our destiny in this hour: *"For the anxious longing of the creation waits eagerly for the revealing of the sons of God"* (Romans 8:19). *"Sons of God"* is a Hebraism that found its way into the original Greek of the New Testament to describe the essential nature of a person. It describes those whose lives can be characterized by the way in which they reflect the character of God Himself.

For at least five decades, the Lord has sown principles of inner healing into the church to bring us to wholeness and holiness. For many of us, life has been a refining fire. Wilderness experiences have been the order of the day, just as they were for Joseph, Moses, David, and even Jesus. God shapes and purifies every one of us who desire His nature and to walk in His will. He does it in whatever way is best for each of us as individuals. All of it works to conform us to the image of the Son to reveal the Father's heart through us in a time when masses of people will be in desperate need of mercy and healing.

"For we know that the whole creation groans and suffers the pains of childbirth together until now" (Romans 8:22, reflective of Matthew 24). The whole of creation travails for the birth of the kingdom of God on earth and the revealing of the sons of God. I believe that a generation of those whose hearts have conformed to the heart of the Father is about to be revealed. Love works. Love conquers. Love attracts. Love and light reveal sin and enable repentance. Do we really believe that light exposes darkness and that the Holy Spirit convicts? If so, then we must love and forgive while the Holy Spirit reveals as darkness what many thought to be light. He brings conviction and repentance.

A CHANGE OF STRATEGY

Even now, God is establishing His presence in regions of refuge. We yet have time to prepare for the inevitable gathering darkness, but only seconds remain on the clock of eternity.

This means that we must deliberately choose passion and purity. Simplicity and love in the Father's heart are the weapons of our conquest. Too many of us in renewal circles have focused on being supernatural. This must stop. It leads to shipwreck. On the other hand, if we will seek intimacy and childlike simplicity with our Father, we will end up being supernatural.

> ## WE ARE NO LONGER A CHRISTIAN CULTURE OR NATION AND WE CANNOT PREVAIL BY OPERATING WITHIN IT ON THAT ASSUMPTION.

We must stop thinking like people who are going to restore something that was. We are no longer a Christian culture or nation and we cannot prevail by operating within it on that assumption. If we insist on that approach, it will only lead us to anger, judgment, and bitterness, alienating people rather than winning their hearts.

For us in the United States, we must realize that in spite of a season of some respite, the Christian America we knew is not coming back, and so we must change both our attitudes and our tactics. We will not gain much ground, or garner the kind of favor Isaiah prophesied, by crying out against sin in a secular world of unbelievers. This only comes across as harsh. We must cry out, not *against* sin, but *for* Jesus, and become the only people in this culture who offer genuine love. As we do this, we must trust that light truly reveals darkness, and that the Holy Spirit truly convicts.

For instance, the early Christians under Rome, the pagan empire that opposed them, knew that they could not call Rome back from something Rome had never known. They knew that they faced a pagan empire. In response, they stood for love in the face of persecution. We must now do the same. We no longer live in a Christian culture. Our tactics must change accordingly. We must learn from history and how the early church did it.

During the Plague of Galen in 165 to 180 AD, Christians were the only ones willing to minister to the sick. While Roman families would cast their own into the street to avoid catching the disease, Christians sent teams to seek out the plague victims and care for them. They were known for love. Light revealed darkness, conviction came, the church grew…and we won.

This points to a change of strategy for us in our day. For the simple reason that they refused to place their hope in anything but Jesus, the early church didn't cry out against the sins of an ungodly culture and an oppressive government. Instead, they proclaimed and demonstrated the reality of God's love and mercy until they turned the heart of an empire.

> RATHER THAN CRYING OUT AGAINST THE SINS OF AN UNGODLY CULTURE, WE MUST PROCLAIM AND DEMONSTRATE THE REALITY OF GOD'S LOVE AND MERCY.

I'm longing for the Josephs and the Daniels to arise, carrying an anointing to speak into national governments and be heard, not because they come as critics, but because they come as servants. I'm longing for a generation of prophets and ordinary believers who will use their supernatural gifts to bless and serve, rather than attack, and who will gain favor and influence because of it. In that spirit, this next outpouring of the Holy Spirit will be one in which Christians who understand the Father's heart and servanthood will rise to positions of influence among the ungodly—kings, rulers, and authorities—where they can demonstrate who the God of heaven really is.

A LAST DAYS MANIFESTO

We are not a *nice* church; we are a powerful people.

We are not a comfortable church; we are a dynamic congregation.

We do not water down the truth; we serve it up full strength.

We do not entertain people; we challenge them to grow and become.

We do not worship to be fed or get something out of it; we worship to touch the heart of God.

We're not there for ourselves; we come for the sake of our brothers and sisters.

We are not *dis*couraged; we are *en*couraged.

We are not power*less*; in Him, we are power*ful*.

We are not *de*stroyed; we are *de*ployed.

United we stand, held in His hand, while feeling our weakness, strong in His greatness.

"Rise and fight! I have given you the land!" declares the Lord of Hosts.

10

BECOMING NATION CHANGERS

Kairos seasons. This biblical Greek word refers to windows in time, *now* moments when God acts in specific ways. *Kairos* is the word Jesus used when He said that Israel did not know the time, the *kairos*, of their visitation. They missed both blessing and destiny when they rejected Him as the Messiah God had sent them. God gave Israel a specific window in time in which to engage and receive the blessing of the kingdom of God in Jesus. The body of Christ stands today on the threshold of one of those *kairos* moments. God is doing something—or is about to—and God's people must wake up and get on board or miss it.

God sent John the Baptist to announce the coming of the kingdom of God and the appearance of the Messiah, and to call God's people to prepare. In just the same way, God now sends reliable prophetic voices to announce that God is about to do something great and to call for preparation. Today, just as in Bible times, we must prepare by means of repentance and a renewed hunger for holiness.

NATION CHANGERS

One key word of the hour in this *kairos* season is *nation changers*. What God is about to do through His people is more than just an outpouring of His Spirit. As governments and cultures ultimately turn to us for answers, this move of God will touch nations and bring favor to His people.

The old charismatic renewal touched the church...but it didn't change nations. The Jesus Movement won hundreds of thousands of young people to the Lord...but it didn't change nations. The Vineyard Movement renewed churches and established the truth that the average believer *could* and *should* minister the power of God...but it didn't change nations.

> MORE THAN ANY MOVE OF GOD THAT CAME BEFORE IT,
> THIS MOVE WILL CHANGE NATIONS.

True, this next move of God will refresh us in the church, and there will be signs and wonders. But more than any move of God that came before it, this move *will* change nations. It will affect governments, schools, businesses, and entire cultures through us who have been filled and gifted with the Spirit of God.

I suspect that most who read these words might have trouble relating to a call to become nation changers. We don't think of ourselves in that way. For most of us, it's enough just to worry about day-to-day life. Changing a nation? Or nations? That might feel like a step too far. Nation-changing therefore gets buried under issues like, "I'm so far behind financially," or "My family is a mess and I don't know what to do," or "My life is so full of going and coming and giving rides to the kids and fixing the car and putting food on the table, I just can't think about some great destiny I never asked for that this crazy pastor is telling me I'm called to."

And yet here it is in 1 Peter 2:9: *"But you are a chosen race, a royal priesthood, a holy nation, a people for God's own possession, so that you may proclaim the excellencies of Him who has called you out of darkness into His marvelous light."* As a people, we have been called and destined to carry a message to the whole world. We are priests, ministers of the gospel, every one of us. We must think of ourselves as pastors in the places where we've been deployed, ministering the power and love of the kingdom of God in every setting and revealing who Jesus really is. As priests of the Lord, we become responsible for the spiritual well-being of those we relate to and touch on a daily basis.

This is neither difficult nor complicated. For example, one brother in my church works as a chef for a senior living facility. Through faithfully serving, he has earned the right to minister the daily devotional over the public address system. Another brother regularly engages people in conversation in places like McDonald's restaurants. He begins by expressing an interest in their lives and then offers to pray for them as they share their hearts. My wife engages the checkers at Walmart, asking them how their lives are going. She earns the right to hear the issues they face in life by simply loving them. On at least one occasion, this resulted in a physical healing. A checker asked her to pray for her mother who was sick with diabetes and in danger of death. Days later, the checker told my wife her mother had been healed.

> ACTS OF LOVE AND COMPASSION SPREAD HOPE WHERE IT'S NEEDED AND OPEN THE DOOR TO SHARING THE TRUTH OF WHO JESUS IS.

These acts of love and compassion spread hope where hope is needed. They open the door to sharing the truth of who Jesus is. We are priests of the Lord, all of us, called to proclaim *"the excellencies of Him who has called"* us. Over time, as these things add up, atmospheres over neighborhoods, workplaces, and cities change. Nations change, one act of mercy added to another.

HEIRS OF ABRAHAM'S PROMISE

The promise to Abraham, father of Israel and father of faith, comes down to us, whether Jew or Gentile, as sons and daughters of Abraham through faith in Jesus. God told Abraham that through his descendants, all of the *nations* of the earth would be blessed. Never did God intend that the promise should be kept to ourselves. It was to affect *all* nations.

The blessing and the promise come to us therefore by inheritance. Our faith in Jesus has included us in the company of the people of God. The promise is ours. We receive it not as a burden or as a heaviness we're forced to carry at the expense of the pleasures of life, but as a blessing. As a blessing, it brings release and joy. Increase and prosperity come with being a blessing to the nations.

God first spoke this promise in Genesis 12, but after the near sacrifice of Abraham's son Isaac, He repeated it in larger terms.

> *Then the angel of the LORD called to Abraham a second time from heaven, and said, "By Myself I have sworn, declares the LORD, because you have done this thing and have not withheld your son, your only son, indeed I will greatly bless you, and I will greatly multiply your seed as the stars of the heavens and as the sand which is on the seashore; and your seed shall possess the gate of their enemies. In your seed all*

the nations of the earth shall be blessed, because you have obeyed My voice." (Genesis 22:15–18)

Clearly, from the very beginning, the gift and calling of God were that we, the people of God, would become much more than just a collection of ordinary people struggling through life like everyone else until the day we go to heaven. God made us to be special. He did this not just for us, but for the sake of the world beyond us. From the start, He destined us for better and greater things, and gifted us with a transcendant purpose, a place of honor, privilege, and authority. Never victims of the world around us, powerless and just surviving, we are a people carrying the power to move the world, to mold it and shape it through the blessing that flows from the Father through us. Never are we to be molded by the world. The world, rather, is to be molded by us.

> **NEVER ARE WE TO BE MOLDED BY THE WORLD. THE WORLD, RATHER, IS TO BE MOLDED BY US.**

The same theme comes up again in Isaiah 60:1–3:

Arise, shine; for your light has come, and the glory of the LORD *has risen upon you. For behold, darkness will cover the earth and deep darkness the peoples; but the* LORD *will rise upon you and His glory will appear upon you. Nations will come to your light, and kings to the brightness of your rising.*

The world remains a bubbling cauldron of trouble and turmoil. Governments are corrupt. Whole societies and cultures stand on the precipice of collapse. Will we, God's people, just sit back and watch it all fall apart as we complain and shield ourselves from it? Or will we awaken to this *kairos* moment and step into the glory appointed for us to change cultures, business structures, education systems, governments, and more?

This is the moment. This is our time. We stand on the threshold of the greatest outpouring of the Spirit of God in human history, our time to step up in glory to shine with the power we've been given to make a difference. Let us become Daniels to the Nebuchadnezzars of our day and Josephs to the Pharaohs of our time. Rather than complain and rebel, Daniel chose to use his gifts to serve the very king who had destroyed his nation and sought to erase his Jewish identity. Pharaoh could in no way have been called a godly king and yet Joseph used his prophetic anointing to serve him. This earned Joseph the number two slot in the kingdom under Pharaoh just in time to save his family from famine.

I SEE THE PROMISE COMING

I see it everywhere I go. As I ministered in Verkhnedneprovsk, Ukraine, they called a young man forward to bless him on his fifteenth birthday. I saw governmental authority all over him, anointing for a destiny to influence his nation in business. As I openly prophesied this, I told him to pursue his education diligently in preparation and not to let anything stop him because he is destined to become a leader to bring integrity to a nation rife with corruption.

The pastor there told me of a woman who dared to run for mayor of her city. To her surprise, she won. My team and I lingered after the service to meet and pray for her, expecting someone old. Instead, we found a beautiful young woman, a mother of children with her husband. She is undoing the culture of corruption and bribes that grip her city, while she endures threats to her life and family from the establishment, but she's making a nation-changing difference.

In Liberia, one of the poorest and most corrupt nations on earth, where I have ministered twice, I'm connected with a young pastor in his early thirties. He has a heart for nation changing. My church and I have invested in him, helping him start a tuition-free school in a nation where education is scarce and costly. Many get no education at all. He has a radio program and frequently confronts his listeners prophetically concerning Jesus, integrity, and morality. He is a nation changer.

I have seen this anointing resting on many in my own congregation. Wherever they go, atmospheres change, hearts are touched, and integrity follows after. Add up all these small pinches of leaven and you eventually see a whole loaf transformed.

AWAKENING A COUNTERCULTURE

It begins with an awakening. While most of the body of Christ remains wrapped in spiritual slumber, a growing remnant is awakening to the voice of God and acting on it. They refuse to listen to the lies of the devil telling them that it can't be done, that they're too small, or that it's a heavy thing, rather than a blessing and a joy.

Every nation on earth has a culture that conditions its people to think, feel, and act in certain ways. Right now, the culture of the western world conditions its people to regard hate as love, immorality as righteousness, rejection of God as freedom, murder of unborn children as defense of women's rights, and a long list of other twisted perceptions. Our government stands paralyzed, families disintegrate, love grows cold, and lawlessness spreads like a cancer. Month after month, we see mass shootings in schools and workplaces. People don't know who they are sexually as men and women. Drugs ravage more lives and homes than at any time in our history.

> TO CREATE A REPLACEMENT COUNTERCULTURE, YOU MUST FIRST BE CHANGED IN YOURSELF. THIS CAN ONLY HAPPEN THROUGH JESUS.

To change a nation, you must first change its culture. To change a culture so that it in turn changes a nation, you must first create a counterculture that moves in a different spirit than the one leading the world to destruction. To create a replacement counterculture, you must first be changed in yourself. This can only happen through Jesus, by His Spirit working in you through repentance, forgiveness, and surrender of old wounds, hurts, and judgments.

> *Now the Lord is the Spirit, and where the Spirit of the Lord is, there is liberty. But we all, with unveiled face, beholding as in a mirror the glory of the Lord, are being transformed into the same image from glory to glory, just as from the Lord, the Spirit.*   (2 Corinthians 3:17–18)

In order for individual transformation to become a culture of transformation, transformed individuals must be joined with others who have been similarly transformed. None of us can do it alone. Culture, by definition, requires a group of people bound together by covenant relationship and common identity. It might start small, first one and then a few, but it becomes the leaven Jesus spoke of. *"He spoke another parable to them, 'The kingdom of heaven is like leaven, which a woman took and hid in three pecks of flour until it was all leavened'"* (Matthew 13:33).

THE EXAMPLE OF SAINT PATRICK

Patrick became a missionary to Ireland in the fifth century when that island was a stronghold of pagan Druidic culture and spirituality. As he won people to faith in Jesus, he gathered them into communities who lived together in love and connection in a culture of the kingdom of God. These communities developed such a reputation for hospitality that travelers across the country would seek them out as way stations on their journeys. Rather than regard these pagan visitors as outsiders, the Celtic Christian communities fathered by Patrick accepted these outsiders as family, including them in meals, times of worship, times of prayer, and Bible study. It was community. It was love. It was covenant. It was profound oneness, a life walked out together. It won the hearts of people and made them believers.

> THE CELTIC CHRISTIAN COMMUNITIES FATHERED BY PATRICK WON THE HEARTS OF PEOPLE AND MADE THEM BELIEVERS.

The Roman expression of the church insisted on convincing people of the rightness of their doctrine in order to make them family. The Celtic Christians in Ireland, however, adopted others into their communities and made them family *first*. Rather than forcing their beliefs on others to *make* them family, they welcomed others *as* family so they came to believe. They drew outsiders into a culture of the kingdom of God, exposed them to something that could be tasted and experienced—a wonderful blending of love and miracles—and changed a nation in the process. It started small, but became a massive transformation. The nation streamed to the brightness of their rising as the leaven of their culture spread, and all they had to do was be themselves in a culture of oneness, honor, love, and unity fed by the Holy Spirit.

TIME TO DECIDE

The church in America and the western world has an urgent decision to make. Will we continue with a situation in which most of the church attends as individuals for an hour a week and then leaves as individuals to lead isolated lives? Or will we become a connected, covenanted family, committed to one another in the Lord to live our lives together as did the church in Acts 2, or the Celtic church in Ireland in the fifth century? By drawing others into genuine family through love and compassion, we can permeate the loaf and win the world, if we choose to do so.

Can we really grasp the truth that we, all of us together, are nation-changers in our connectedness as we're deployed into our various arenas of life, whether we work flipping burgers in a fast-food franchise, or occupy some high government position? Collectively, God has called us to be a counterculture of the kingdom of God. Individually, we are pinches of leaven sown into the flour of the world to multiply and change the nature of the lump by who and what we are.

> INDIVIDUALLY, WE ARE PINCHES OF LEAVEN SOWN INTO THE FLOUR OF THE WORLD, TO BRING A COUNTERCULTURE OF THE KINGDOM OF GOD.

We change atmospheres in homes, at work, neighborhoods, and schools. There is no darkness anywhere we go because darkness can never overcome light. Jesus taught us that we are the light of the world and light up the world around us. (See Matthew 5:14.) You might protest and lament that the place where you live or work is so full of darkness…but you'd be wrong. You *are* the light of the world, and where you go, light removes darkness. That dark place ceased to be dark the moment you entered it.

When you come into a loveless place, love comes with you. Power and authority come with you when you walk into that situation in which you feel helpless and where you sense people laboring under oppression. When you walk into any room, demons tremble because the Lord of life is in you. When you come into any broken place, healing comes with you because the Healer dwells in you.

As I say this, I'm certainly not advising anyone to have faith in themselves. I know where that goes. Eventually, I'll let even myself down, and then I'll let all of you down. I'm telling you to believe in the One who dwells in you. Rest in Him. Walk in Him. Let Him shine.

You are from God, little children, and have overcome them; because greater is He who is in you than he who is in the world. (1 John 4:4)

IT TAKES A CULTURE

A core value we practice in the church I pastor is, "Good shepherding gives the sheep that which is their own." In 1 Corinthians 12:7, the apostle Paul wrote that each one has been gifted for the common good. Part of building toward this nation-changing culture is that we cultivate an atmosphere of such love and freedom that it activates and calls forth what God has put in each believer. We're not building a great ministry empire with someone's name on it, asking all of you to fit into it for the greater glory of those of us in leadership.

The glory is that God has put His Spirit into every one of us who has received Jesus as Lord and Savior. He has seeded His dreams and hopes into the hearts of all those He has called to Himself. With those dreams and hopes come supernatural strength and ability to truly love and bring change to lives. Then, when it all adds up collectively, we change nations by changing the cultures of nations. But it begins with the culture of each individual home, then each community and workplace. Leaven is alive. It grows until it changes the very nature of the lump of dough into which it has been placed.

Who has He created *you* to be? What burns in your spirit? Do you have a dream? Is there something you'd like to see happen in the kingdom of God? Have you longed to touch the world outside the church in some godly and holy way? This nation-changing culture calls that up and gives it a place to grow. It sets you free to fly and equips you to do it. Have we been equipping people only to be good church members, ministering within the safe confines of an essentially closed circle, giving to and supporting the church, while forgetting that some among us carry dreams, gifts, and callings to rock the world outside?

My own church has a food pantry because it was birthed in the heart of one of our older members living on Social Security Disability. A dream became reality. We have a Sunday morning café serving an affordable breakfast, with the proceeds supporting missions, because someone had a dream and we enabled him to make it happen. Our church has an effective men's ministry because it was born in the heart of a man who chose to seek out other men and draw them together. A group focused on recovery from addictions is developing because God put it into the heart of one of our couples. As a church, we facilitated these dreams and gave them room to grow.

> THE CHURCH NEEDS A CULTURE THAT RELEASES WHAT GOD HAS PLACED IN EACH INDIVIDUAL MEMBER.

The church needs a culture that releases what God has placed in each individual member. In my own congregation, we then put the resources of the church behind helping our people to realize the dreams God has already birthed in them. It's a culture of honor, covenant, and relationship. It's a culture of real grace. We want to give our people what God has said is theirs, activating them in the Lord. Some will be called to the internal ministries of the church. Others will be fed and supported by the base the local church provides, but their sphere of influence will be in the wider world.

The early church, in the first three centuries after Jesus ascended into heaven, changed the Roman world and won the empire through the culture of love and honor that came into existence on the day of Pentecost. They were nation-changers. We, the remnant, have come into a *kairos* season when the church must once more become culture-builders and changers of nations all around the world. We stand at the threshold, the beginning, of that release.

REVIVAL APPLIED

I've long said that the revival to come will be different, not a repeat of what has gone before. In the past, I knew only that it would bring a deeper and purer focus on Jesus, as well as an emphasis on wholeness and holiness. I know now that the time has come for the fulfillment of Isaiah 60, that nations and kings would stream to the brightness of our rising. It's time for the Josephs and Daniels of our day to rise, exert influence, and gain favor with kings, governors, business executives, and ordinary bosses—the power brokers of our day.

Those of us who call ourselves by the name of Jesus Christ must develop a reputation as the most reliable, most desirable employees in the nation, the most helpful and excellent craftsmen, and the most honest businessmen and women. Our name must come to be associated with a reputation as peacemakers and healers, the go-to people when solutions are needed. These things build credibility. These things earn us the right to speak and be heard in a culture that doesn't understand the core of our faith.

When you've prayed for a neighbor and they sense God and experience a healing, and they say, "What was that?" then culture begins to change. You've sown a pinch of leaven. When you've sensed in the spirit some problem, obstacle, or opportunity that might be coming to your boss, and you inform him or her while providing a solution, and they say, "How did you know?" the lump of dough begins to change as your influence and favor increase.

When the power brokers in your life feel the grace flowing from you while everyone else complains and criticizes, and they ask, "What is so different about you?" the leaven begins to multiply. Favor begins to flow. This is how leaven works. It begins as a pinch but grows to permeate the whole lump of dough, changing it visibly for the better.

There's nothing difficult about it. Just walk with Jesus and be who He has made you to be.

11

THE TRUTH ABOUT PENTECOST

THE PROMISE

Gathering them together, He commanded them not to leave Jerusalem, but to wait for what the Father had promised, "Which," He said, "you heard of from Me; for John baptized with water, but you will be baptized with the Holy Spirit not many days from now." So when they had come together, they were asking Him, saying, "Lord, is it at this time You are restoring the kingdom to Israel?" He said to them, "It is not for you to know times or epochs which the Father has fixed by His own authority; but you will receive power when the Holy Spirit has come upon you; and you shall be My witnesses both in Jerusalem, and in all Judea and Samaria, and even to the remotest part of the earth." And after He had said these things, He was lifted up while

they were looking on, and a cloud received Him out of their
sight.   (Acts 1:4–9)

THE FULFILLMENT

When the day of Pentecost had come, they were all together
in one place. And suddenly there came from heaven a
noise like a violent rushing wind, and it filled the whole
house where they were sitting. And there appeared to them
tongues as of fire distributing themselves, and they rested
on each one of them. And they were all filled with the Holy
Spirit and began to speak with other tongues, as the Spirit
was giving them utterance. Now there were Jews living in
Jerusalem, devout men from every nation under heaven.
And when this sound occurred, the crowd came together,
and were bewildered because each one of them was hearing
them speak in his own language. They were amazed and
astonished, saying, "Why, are not all these who are speak-
ing Galileans? And how is it that we each hear them in our
own language to which we were born? Parthians and Medes
and Elamites, and residents of Mesopotamia, Judea and
Cappadocia, Pontus and Asia, Phrygia and Pamphylia,
Egypt and the districts of Libya around Cyrene, and visitors
from Rome, both Jews and proselytes, Cretans and Arabs—
we hear them in our own tongues speaking of the mighty
deeds of God." And they all continued in amazement and
great perplexity, saying to one another, "What does this
mean?" But others were mocking and saying, "They are full
of sweet wine."   (Acts 2:1–13)

Aside from the crucifixion and resurrection of Jesus, the
most important day in the history of the church is the day

of Pentecost, but it is also the most misunderstood and even neglected. Also called *Shavuot*, it was and is one of the three compulsory feasts of Judaism. In Bible times, the Law required every able-bodied Jewish male to make the journey to Jerusalem at *Shavuot* to appear before the Lord at the temple. Celebrated fifty days after Passover, it commemorates the giving of the Law at Mount Sinai during the exodus from slavery in Egypt. It was also a harvest festival, a time to offer first fruits of the field to the Lord.

> ASIDE FROM THE CRUCIFIXION AND RESURRECTION OF JESUS, PENTECOST IS THE MOST IMPORTANT DAY IN CHURCH HISTORY— BUT IT'S ALSO THE MOST MISUNDERSTOOD AND EVEN NEGLECTED.

Travel would have been easier at Pentecost, which happened later in the spring, than during the season of Passover. That made it perhaps the best attended of the feasts, which meant there were a great many people in the city when the Holy Spirit fell on the church in power. Tens of thousands would have crowded the streets so that when Peter stood up to preach, three thousand men and their families heard and came to believe in Jesus.

THE POINT OF THE OUTPOURING

What was the real point of Pentecost? Why did God gift them and us with His power? I tend to think the body of Christ has often been somewhat confused about this. At least since the Azusa Street revival in 1906, Christians who believe in the gifts of the Spirit have tended to focus in an unbalanced way on speaking in tongues. The goal seemed to be to get people blasted by the Holy Spirit and speaking in tongues, then, whammo! You're baptized in the Spirit!

As I grew up in the charismatic renewal, I remember being surrounded by a crowd of people in my father's living room, picking at me like the seagulls in the movie, *Finding Nemo*, crying, "Mine! Mine! Mine!" as they went after poor little Nemo. These people kept telling me it was just on the tip of my tongue if I would only let it out. They were wrong. I felt nothing but pressure coming from them, but they were desperate to get me speaking in tongues. I was sixteen years old at the time and couldn't wait to get away from them. I actually did receive the gift of tongues years later, but at sixteen, I just wanted to escape the pressure. Wrong focus results in poor fruit and even violation.

> REAL BAPTISM IN THE SPIRIT IS ABOUT POWER AND WITNESS.

TWO KEY WORDS

Two key words in what Jesus promised His disciples define what real baptism in the Spirit is about: *power* and *witness*. Jesus said, *"You will receive power when the Holy Spirit has come upon you; and you shall be My witnesses."*

The Holy Spirit impacted them so strongly in Acts 2, they staggered around as if drunk, and, yes, they received the gift of tongues. Being drunk in the Spirit was simply the inability of the human body to absorb all that God was giving without some kind of effect. In short, they couldn't hold their spiritual liquor. Good times! The power of God cannot be controlled, but more than just giving us an experience of God, it fills us with the purposes of God.

The gift of tongues was released initially as a means of allowing Jews who had gathered from all over the world for the feast of Pentecost to hear God's praises in their native tongues spoken miraculously by Galileeans who couldn't possibly have known those languages. It enabled those people to believe.

Later, the gift of tongues became more than merely miraculous praise intended for witnessing. In 1 Corinthians 14, the apostle Paul defined it as a gift for prayer and personal edification. (See 1 Corinthians 14:2, 4.) When used in a church setting openly, a prayer uttered in tongues needed to be accompanied by the gift of interpretation so that everyone could add the amen to what was prayed in tongues. Initially, however, it fell under the heading of *witness,* a tool for sharing who Jesus is and what He has done.

God voiced the promise of power three times in the biblical record.

The first was Joel 2:28–32:

> *It will come about after this that I will pour out My Spirit on all mankind; and your sons and daughters will prophesy, your old men will dream dreams, your young men will see visions. Even on the male and female servants I will pour out My Spirit in those days. I will display wonders in the sky and on the earth, blood, fire and columns of smoke. The sun will be turned into darkness and the moon into blood before the great and awesome day of the LORD comes. And it will come about that whoever calls on the name of the LORD will be delivered.*

Peter stood up to preach on the day of Penecost and declared that what they were seeing that day was a fulfillment of what Joel had prophesied.

The second record of the promise of power through baptism in the Spirit is found in Matthew 3:11 when John the Baptist preached to prepare the people for the time when Jesus would emerge and bring the kingdom of God to earth: *"As for me, I baptize you with water for repentance, but He who is coming after me is mightier than I, and I am not fit to remove His sandals; He will baptize you with the Holy Spirit and fire."*

Scripture reports the third time in Acts 1 where Jesus told them to wait for the power the Father had promised. Two key words: *power* for *witness*.

> ## OUR BAPTISM IN THE HOLY SPIRIT IS CENTRAL TO GOD'S HEART IN HIS DESIRES FOR US.

NOT AN OPTION

Can you sense how important this baptism is to God? It's not an option, nor do we get to pick and choose whether we like it or want it to be part of our lives. It seems pretty central to God's heart in His desires for us. We cannot and must not reject it merely because it makes us uncomfortable, goes beyond the boundaries of our understanding, or transcends our ability to control it. It comes full of glory, but is seldom comfortable or even orderly in man's terms. God didn't call us to be comfortable or to fill our churches by entertaining the masses. He didn't call us to cater to a culture out of fear of offending someone or threatening someone's lifestyle.

He called us, rather, to bear witness to who He is and to manifest His rule and reign, His kingdom, here on earth. Baptism in the Spirit empowers us to do that. He didn't call us to do it as a labor, but to do it because we've been so impacted by the Spirit of God, so filled with Him, that we can't help but do it. Therein lies the heart of the promise!

THE MOST IMPORTANT THING

On the day of Pentecost, the most important thing was not the gift of tongues or the fact that they were so overcome with the Holy Spirit that they staggered around like drunks. The most important thing was that the infilling they received transformed them from a company of cowards, hiding out in the upper room for fear of the Jews, into an army of fearless witnesses for Jesus willing to take floggings for Him and walk away full of joy for the opportunity to share Jesus and to share in His sufferings.

And all for the sake of making disciples of all nations. He didn't call us to put butts in the seats or to grow the church. He called us to make disciples. He called us to bear such a witness for the truth of who Jesus is through our transformed lives that it would dramatically transform the lives of others so that they would reflect and walk in the nature of Jesus Himself.

Baptism in the Spirit turned the deacon Stephen into not just a worker of signs and wonders, but into someone who could preach to a hostile crowd and continue preaching, even while being stoned to death. It transformed a young man named Saul from one filled with murderous hatred for Christians into a man who would fearlessly and willingly pay any price to bear witness to what he knew of Jesus, the very one he'd been trying stamp out. By his own testimony, he was *"beaten times without number, often in danger of death. Five times I received from the Jews thirty-nine lashes. Three times I was beaten with rods, once I was stoned, three times I was shipwrecked, a night and a day I have spent in the deep"* (2 Corinthians 11:23–25).

Baptism in the Spirit turned a group of people who had not known one another—who came from all over the Roman world for the feast of Pentecost, speaking different languages—into a group of people so in love with the Lord and with one another that they began selling their possessions in order to share with those among them who had need. I believe that those who had come from great distances to celebrate Pentecost, and then became Spirit-baptized believers in Jesus, didn't want to leave to go back home. They stayed for the glory poured out, but they had no means of support, having left jobs and businesses behind. The church therefore rallied as one in love to meet the need. *Love. "And the Lord was adding to their number day by day those who were being saved"* (Acts 2:47).

Every sacrifice that followed after the baptism in the Spirit was for the sake of making disciples of all nations. Jesus didn't call us to make sure the pews were full. He called us to make disciples, to recreate in others what He has done in us.

> JESUS CALLED US TO MAKE DISCIPLES,
> TO RECREATE IN OTHERS WHAT HE HAS DONE IN US.

IMMERSED IN THE SPIRIT

Baptism, by definition, is immersion. This means you're all-in, not just dabbling your toes, checking it out, or merely getting splashed with the Spirit for the sake of a nice experience. The Greek word means *immersed*. It's so much more than being filled, and it goes well beyond being just a wonderful personal experience. To be baptized in the Holy Spirit is to be surrounded by, covered by, and saturated by the Spirit of God in power to witness for Jesus so that His love and His mission become your whole world. In the baptism in the Spirit, this happens not because you worked at it as some kind of legalism, or because the pastor made you feel guilty for failing to share your faith openly. When you've been baptized in the Spirit along with your brothers and sisters, it's a natural overflow.

At Pentecost, the Holy Spirit hit them in the upper room with such force that they couldn't stay inside. It wasn't some nice comfortable worship service safely hidden in a building where no one else could see them. No one told them to go out and preach. They literally could not stop themselves. There they were, in full view of thousands, speaking in tongues for all to hear, not because some preacher told them they had to do it, but because what they had just been given had to find expression in overflow.

SIDE EFFECTS

Baptism in the Spirit does come with side effects. You might get drunk in the Spirit, fall on the floor and shake, or speak in tongues. You might lose control and laugh until your abdominal muscles ache the next day. Wonderful! I love it when God makes a mess! But the side effects are neither the promise nor the substance. The substance of the promise finds expression in those two words: *power* and *witness*. The promise itself is that we get to be part of an ever-expanding influence for Jesus, changing cultures and changing nations. Jesus told His disciples it would be Jerusalem, Judea, Samaria, and the ends of the earth.

GIFT, NOT LEGALISM

You can be captivated by the religious spirit, miss it, and think that when Jesus said, *"You shall be my witnesses,"* He was saying you *must* be My witnesses. In reality, He gave no command, but rather promised power and privilege. He meant that when you receive this power, you will do and be these things because the impact of being immersed in His Spirit changes you. It transforms.

You receive the baptism in the Spirit because you've said yes to a destiny, a purpose beyond yourself. It is the gift of our Father who loves His sons and daughters beyond measure and gives them destiny, purpose, and meaning.

Sometimes, we do have decisions to make. Promises tend to come to pass when they're acted on. Something incredibly powerful has been given to you and you've been filled with it. Now, will you make a decision to open the floodgates and allow what has filled you to get out? Will you tap into it and let it show? Will you decide to let it effectively get out of control?

With everything in me, I believe that God is about to send and release the greatest move of the Spirit since the day of Pentecost. I believe this move of God to be the end times outpouring, greater and more far-reaching than Pentecost ever could have been.

NATION-CHANGING POWER

Where previous moves of God have renewed the church but done little to affect nations, the coming move is nation-changing. It will include the rise of Josephs and Daniels who affect kings and rulers as they employ their spiritual gifts to influence authorities to shape nations.

It will be a last-days fulfillment of Isaiah 60:2–3: *"For behold, darkness will cover the earth and deep darkness the peoples; but the LORD will rise upon you and His glory will appear upon you. Nations will come to your light, and kings to the brightness of your rising."* Purity of focus on Jesus will be the hallmark.

PREPARING FOR THE OUTPOURING

For five decades, our Lord has sown inner healing tools into the body of Christ in order to prepare a generation to walk safely in wholeness and rest in that outpouring. Inner healing—better described as transformation—was never intended to be primarily remedial. Rather, it prepares us for glory. Rooted in confession, repentance, and the cross of Jesus, real inner healing calls for cleansing of impurity and for death to self for the sake of others. In the same way that John the Baptist announced the coming of Jesus and the nearness of the kingdom of God by calling for repentance, so the prophetic cry goes forth today. We prepare to receive and be part of this outpouring by seeking wholeness and holiness.

> REAL INNER HEALING CALLS FOR CLEANSING OF IMPURITY AND FOR DEATH TO SELF FOR THE SAKE OF OTHERS.

We all know the obvious traditional issues of repentance—turning away from fornication and adultery, dishonesty, or drug addiction, for instance—but this goes deeper. Maybe it's things like:

Lord, I've been asleep spiritually.
Lord, I've allowed the pain of life to make me self-centered.
I've judged Your people.
I've not kept my relationships whole.
I've not seen You, Lord, for who You are.
Lord, my insecurities have polluted my relationships and hindered my witness for You. It's made me ambitious instead of humble.
I've been seeking to validate me rather than reveal You.
Lord, I see destructive patterns in my life and I want them gone.

Lord, I've nursed my wounds instead of seeking healing and they've infected and hindered my relationship with You and with people and my effect on the kingdom. Lord, some of my relationships are broken and I've not done all I can to heal them.

THE CENTRALITY OF PRAYER

Jesus instructed them to wait in Jerusalem for the promise of receiving the power, but in Scripture, the command to wait almost never means to do nothing. More often, it calls us to press in to God, to seek His Presence, to turn toward Him with a singular focus. In Acts 1, they therefore prayed for ten days while they waited, beginning with the twelve and increasing to the one hundred and twenty. I think and know that they spent significant portions of that time in cleansing and repentance. As with John the Baptist's call to prepare, so it was then...and so it is now.

Accordingly, in John 20, prior to the day of Pentecost, Jesus breathed on them to impart authority over sin.

And when He had said this, He breathed on them and said to them, "Receive the Holy Spirit. If you forgive the sins of any, their sins have been forgiven them; if you retain the sins of any, they have been retained."   (John 20:22–23)

In the Greek, *retained* carries the sense of *to seize and hurl.* This was power and authority to overcome sin and cast it away. Doesn't it seem obvious that they would have acted on that anointing as they waited for the promise? As they faced and dealt with sin, brokenness, and relational pollutions, they came to a place of unity unlike any they had ever experienced.

*"These all **with one mind** were continually devoting themselves to prayer, along with the women, and Mary the mother of Jesus, and with His brothers"* (Acts 1:14). I like to think this implies that they were not just in one physical place, but that they were deeply united in heart and spirit. Notice the key words, *"with one mind."* Singular focus, with clean hearts toward one another, prepared them to receive the promised outpouring. They stood together passionately in agreement concerning the goal and the purpose so that they were prepared to receive.

> SINGULAR FOCUS, WITH CLEAN HEARTS TOWARD ONE ANOTHER, PREPARED THE DISCIPLES TO RECEIVE THE PROMISED OUTPOURING.

For ten days, from the ascension of Jesus to the day of Pentecost, they prayed in agreement with unified passion for what the Father had promised, preparing for the coming power and laying the foundation, until they stood in purity and unity.

> *When the day of Pentecost had come, they were all together in one place. And suddenly there came from heaven a noise like a violent rushing wind, and it filled the whole house where they were sitting. And there appeared to them tongues as of fire distributing themselves, and they rested on each one of them.* (Acts 2:1–3)

Then came the side effects, the manifestations to which so many critics object. Peter spoke up:

> *For these men are not drunk, as you suppose, for it is only the third hour of the day; but this is what was spoken of through the prophet Joel: "And it shall be in the last days," God says, "that I will pour forth of My Spirit on all mankind; and your sons and your daughters shall prophesy, and your young men shall see visions, and your old men*

shall dream dreams; even on My bondslaves, both men and
women, I will in those days pour forth of My Spirit and they
shall prophesy. And I will grant wonders in the sky above
and signs on the earth below, blood, and fire, and vapor of
smoke. The sun will be turned into darkness and the moon
into blood, before the great and glorious day of the Lord
shall come. And it shall be that everyone who calls on the
name of the Lord will be saved."   (Acts 2:15–21)

As the Holy Spirit empowered them, they made disciples. This didn't mean getting them to say the sinner's prayer at the altar in order to receive their tickets to heaven with permission to go on about their business. As disciples, they worshiped daily together in the temple and met from house to house, enjoying meals together and sitting under the apostles' teaching. They shared everything they had and cared for the poor in their midst.

In other words, they lived *disciple* things together, not as a religious exercise or a labor, but because they had received power in the Holy Spirit to do it. The world saw the beauty of it and streamed to them. *"And the Lord was adding to their number day by day those who were being saved"* (Acts 2:47).

WHEN YOU RECEIVE

When you receive the Holy Spirit, you're receiving not just an experience, but the very Person of God. With Him come His values, His goals, His purposes, and His nature. If you will listen to Him and yield to His Spirit at every level of your being, you're in for the time of your life.

Holiness is the word of the hour, but it's not about all the things we *don't* do. It's all the wonderful things we do *instead*. It's about the things we are privileged to be *allowed* to do. Holiness doesn't start with our own efforts at perfection. It starts with

His holiness and His perfection. It starts at the cross where He became the pure, sinless, and undefiled sacrifice for our sin. It doesn't start with *our* passion for Him. It starts with *His* passion for us. It doesn't start with whether or not *we* love God hard enough. He loves *us* hard enough. We have only to respond!

Holiness doesn't start with our wholeness, or getting over our brokenness, our strongholds and judgments, expectations, demons, and addictions. It starts with His perfection and the righteousness He pours out on us as a gift. Our responsibility is to receive it, surrender to it, and live it.

> HOLINESS DOESN'T START WITH US;
> IT STARTS WITH HIS PERFECTION AND THE RIGHTEOUSNESS HE
> POURS OUT ON US AS A GIFT.

When we as a people get baptized, immersed in the Spirit, things change. We change. The comfortable boring life we may have known comes to an end and the adventure begins with all the risks and all the fun.

God is not calling you and filling you with His Spirit because you're strong enough, holy enough, good enough, or sufficiently filled with passion. Every one of those people filled on the day of Pentecost had been a mess. Peter, James, and John fell asleep in Gethsemane the night before the crucifixion when Jesus needed them the most. Later that night, Peter denied Jesus three times. After Jesus had been raised from the dead, Peter left the ministry to return to fishing. Jesus rebuked him and ordered him to pick it up again. Thomas refused to believe the testimony of those who had seen the risen Jesus until he could actually touch the Lord with his hands. They'd fought among themselves over who was the greatest. They were a mess. Consequently, they had plenty to pray about during those ten days.

He's not calling you because you're ready or perfect, any more than He called the original disciples because they were ready or perfect. You're none of that and neither am I. I'm a pastor today only because God closed every other door and *made* me do this. So, when the baptism in the Spirit comes, God does great things through weak and broken you. He gets the glory for it, while you get to have all the fun. He's doing it because He loves you.

God has never been interested in calling you to do what you *can* do. What would be the point in that? He's the Creator. He spoke the universe into being. Calling you to do what you *can* do wouldn't be any fun. He's truly interested, however, in asking you to do things you *can't* do, things you can do only if He does them in and through you. He starts with the least and makes it the most. Small things don't bother Him because He's a God of increase and multiplication. He wants to extend Himself through you. You're never ready for that. You will never feel adequate. You're never strong enough, good enough, holy enough, talented enough, smart enough, gifted or spiritual enough. But in the baptism in the Spirit, you're filled, empowered, and sent on an adventure.

I want to see a people immersed in God's Spirit, experiencing more of God than they ever have in their lives, and then rising up to do, not what we're comfortable with, and not what we *can* do, but what we cannot do without Him.

12

WHY I CAN'T PRAY FOR REVIVAL

Among those truly passionate for Jesus, I hear a growing hunger and rising cry for the Lord to send revival. I understand what we mean by that. An expanding remnant longs ever more deeply after the genuine experience of God. They're tired of routine, tired of hype, tired of pretense, and tired of being manipulated. They grow weary of the generally shallow presentations they often hear on Christian television. They no longer have patience with the methods they're told will produce prosperity or blessing that mostly fail to produce what they promise. Nothing less than depth of heart and spirit will satisfy them, and so they cry for revival because they don't know what else to do. They hear prophetic voices prophesying the great revival to come, igniting hope, and they seek the genuine.

Too often, however, this longing comes with a package of expectations and a list of things we want to see and experience.

Too often we associate it—or even equate it—with laughing, falling, shaking, roaring, prophecies, speaking in tongues, and miracles of various kinds. *Hey! Jesus was really moving! Everybody fell down!* Or we see it too narrowly, minus the manifestations, as people coming to Jesus and getting saved. Getting saved is a great thing. Salvations *do* increase when revival is real. All good and OK! These things are wonderful and genuine. So, whatever our expectations might be, we pray, *Lord send revival!*

All the same, I think that the majority of folks don't really care about most of that. Instead, what they *really* care about is everyday life. Getting the bills paid. Dealing with a failing marriage. Surviving cancer. Finding an affordable place to live. *Who's going to care for the kids while Mom is at work?* Or, *I'm getting old—how will I live when I can't work anymore?* Or perhaps, *I'm young but I'm an adult now and life is here, so how will I live? Can I afford to get an education? Or am I stuck in this drone of a job I hate?*

God cares about all those things. He takes no joy in the struggles His kids go through. But that's not the focus of where He's taking us. Remember Matthew 6:33: *"But seek first His kingdom and His righteousness, and all these things will be added to you."* This is usually one of the first verses with a promise every new believer learns…and I suspect it's one of the first we tend to forget when life comes down on us.

Do we need revival? Absolutely! Because when we wake up out of spiritual slumber and respond to the Holy Spirit, people do come to Him, families get healed, sickness goes, and cultures change. Problems find resolution.

I CAN'T PRAY FOR REVIVAL

Strangely, however, for years now, God hasn't allowed me to pray for revival. I want to explain why, at least as I understand it. I believe I'm being told to lay down my revival paradigm, the things I've seen happen and have come to expect, as well as the things I want to see happen. God has told me to burn the list and surrender the expectations I would measure it by. I've talked to a number of folks who've given up hope because the list they identified with revival—the cry for a move of God—didn't seem to be heard in heaven. Too much time had passed and it appeared that nothing was happening.

The problem with lists of expectations is that they can blind us to what God is really doing, especially if we're praying in the wrong direction. These paradigms and expectations can actually constitute demands we make on God that potentially render us insensitive to what He is actually doing. They set us up for disappointment when we don't see what we want to see. It's as though we're saying, "There's nothing checked off on my shopping list of desires for my life, my church, and my experience. God must not be doing anything." And then we get hurt, discouraged, or just plain angry.

> GOD IS SAYING TO STOP PRAYING FOR SPECIFIC RESULTS AND SIMPLY LEARN TO TRUST.

On so many fronts, God is saying to stop praying for specific results and simply learn to trust. There's a difference between having faith *for* some specific outcome and having faith *in* Jesus, who never lets us down. Faith *for* something can lead down a dark path because it focuses us on an eventuality we want to see, instead of the Person of Jesus, who brings the better outcome we might not even have imagined. Faith *in* Jesus opens the way to following Jesus into peace and glory because He gives what is right and appropriate beyond anything you or I could think up.

REVIVAL PRAYERS IN THE BIBLE?

It might sound odd, but I don't see anyone praying for revival in the scriptural record of the book of Acts. Go back to the beginning, to the day of Pentecost, when the power of the Holy Spirit fell on the one hundred and twenty in the upper room and filled them for the first time. They spoke in foreign tongues, languages they had never learned, and then won three thousand men with their families to the Lord in just one day.

> *Gathering them together, He commanded them not to leave Jerusalem, but to wait for what the Father had promised, "Which," He said, "you heard of from Me; for John baptized with water, but you will be baptized with the Holy Spirit not many days from now."* (Acts 1:4–5)

On Ascension Day, Jesus didn't tell them to *pray* for anything at all. He'd already taught them to pray for the kingdom to come, for the Father's will to be done on earth as in heaven, but this was different. Something was about to break upon them in power—the actual kingdom come to earth—God's will done here, just as in heaven.

WAITING FOR THE PROMISE

Jesus gave them a command with a promise. He told them to wait, and He promised power: *"But you will receive power when the Holy Spirit has come upon you; and you shall be My witnesses both in Jerusalem, and in all Judea and Samaria, and even to the remotest part of the earth"* (Acts 1:8).

It's important to realize that everything Jesus said and taught was steeped in the Old Testament Scriptures that both He and the people knew. What we call the Old Testament was *all* they knew, and the New Testament is peppered with quotes from it. The disciples themselves had been schooled in the Law, the prophets, and the writings from childhood.

When He said to wait, therefore, I can't help but think that He had Isaiah 40 in mind and that the disciples would have readily dialed it up:

> *Yet those who wait for the LORD will gain new strength; they will mount up with wings like eagles, they will run and not get tired, they will walk and not become weary.*
> (Isaiah 40:31)

To wait on the Lord is to stop, sit down, still your heart and mind, and be silent until God says to speak or move. As you wait, the flesh begins to lose its force and wither away. It means telling your spirit, your heart, and your mind to stop and be still. *"Tremble, and do not sin; meditate in your heart upon your bed, and be still. Selah. Offer the sacrifices of righteousness, and trust in the LORD"* (Psalm 4:4–5).

> TO WAIT ON THE LORD IS TO STOP, SIT DOWN, STILL YOUR HEART AND MIND, AND BE SILENT UNTIL GOD SAYS TO SPEAK OR MOVE.

Ten days passed between the ascension of Jesus into heaven and the feast of Pentecost. Because Jesus didn't tell them how long to wait, they had no idea how long it would be, but they understood that *wait* didn't mean to twiddle their thumbs and do nothing. Although waiting includes being still and listening, it isn't actually a time for inactivity. While we wait, we prepare. I know they spent those days in prayer preparing because Acts 1 tells us they prayed and that the numbers who had gathered swelled to one hundred and twenty by the time the Spirit fell on them. They knew that, in order to prepare, they needed to devote themselves to prayer. What else would they do?

During those ten days, what was the agenda, if there was one? As I have already pointed out in this book, I believe they prepared a platform strong enough, alert and alive enough, to bear or contain the power Jesus had promised them. God is wise. He knows that you don't pump the gasoline until you have a tank to put it in. You don't wait until the baby is a week old to have the diapers ready and the crib in place. In order to receive, you need a container ready to receive. I believe, however, that there is another level to it.

> WHEN WE PRAY FOR REVIVAL, WE'RE ACTUALLY BEGGING FOR A PROMISED GIFT THAT'S ALREADY BEEN GIVEN. INSTEAD, WE SHOULD PRAY FOR AWAKENING.

THE NEEDED AWAKENING TO RECEIVE

Praying for revival is praying for a move of God, but because Jesus had already promised a move of God, it was already established and made certain. I therefore believe that when you and I pray for revival, we're actually begging for a promised gift that's already been given. Instead, we should pray for awakening. We must cry to be awakened from spiritual slumber, that we might come out of our caves and coverings and all that has lulled us to sleep or dulled our senses. We must cry to be enabled to receive what God has already sent, already promised, and already established.

MORE ON PREPARATION

In those ten days between the ascension and Pentecost, I don't believe they were praying for revival as we understand revival. I don't believe they were praying for the Spirit to be poured out, or for the power to come. Jesus had already promised these; it was already a certainty, not something they needed to beg for. They had only to wait...but in waiting, there is preparation.

If you don't sand a rough wooden surface before you paint, the paint won't stick. If you build a house before the foundation has been poured, the house can't stand. So, yes, the disciples were waiting and, according to the Scriptures available to them at the time, waiting meant trusting. Waiting means not working or striving to make anything happen. To wait is to stop and trust, but it also calls for dealing with anything that would obstruct rest and trust. Whatever might form a barrier to receiving the gift of God must be faced and settled.

At least for the twelve, as I have already pointed out, in the days leading up to Pentecost, there would have been relationship issues accumulated through three and half years of walking with Jesus in close fellowship with one another. The pressure of ministry, as well as off-target expectations, triggered issues of the heart, attitudes, and fears. The first chapter of Acts doesn't give us a list, but in John 20, when Jesus appeared to them after He had been raised, we get a strong hint of what must have come up.

> So Jesus said to them again, "Peace be with you; as the Father has sent Me, I also send you." And when He had said this, He breathed on them and said to them, "Receive the Holy Spirit. If you forgive the sins of any, their sins have been forgiven them; if you retain the sins of any, they have been retained." (John 20:21–23)

One could surmise that one lingering ungodly element was a lack of peace among the disciples in their relationships. As I have already pointed out, the original Greek for *retain* actually means something like *to seize and hurl*—authority and power to cast sin and brokenness away as it is exposed.

> **THE SECOND INFILLING OF THE SPIRIT GIFTED THE DISCIPLES WITH POWER TO CARRY THE WORD OF JESUS INTO THE WORLD AND DEMONSTRATE THE KINGDOM OF GOD FOR ALL TO SEE.**

It seems clear that Scripture speaks of two impartations of the Holy Spirit. First came a preliminary one that filled them with the Holy Spirit for authority to deal with brokenness and impurity. Jesus breathed the Spirit into them in order to empower them to prepare for the second infilling. The second infilling of the Spirit gifted them with power to carry the word about Jesus into the world and demonstrate the kingdom of God, the Father's heart, and His love in tangible ways for the world to see. But before the second outpouring could come and remain, there had to be a solid foundation for it to rest upon. In order to receive what God was about to send, that which hindered had to be removed and a container capable of holding it had to be made whole.

In John 20, therefore, the inbreathing of the Holy Spirit enabled and empowered them to begin to establish that foundation. *"If you forgive the sins of any, their sins have been forgiven them; if you retain the sins of any, they have been retained."* He gave them power and authority to forgive as well as power and authority to conquer the unholy within them, to put it away and be done with it.

Authority to forgive and to truly love comes from Jesus and has been imparted into us as believers. When we received Jesus, He gave us that authority in His Spirit. We are not helpless. We are not victims of our circumstances or the sins committed against us. More importantly, the inbreathing of the Spirit involved allowing the Holy Spirit to expose and reveal what was dark or unholy in them, beyond forgiving others and beyond repenting of the traditional sin list of violations and immoral acts.

> **AUTHORITY TO FORGIVE AND TO TRULY LOVE COMES FROM JESUS AND HAS BEEN IMPARTED INTO US AS BELIEVERS.**

In my own case, I don't drink, I don't smoke, and I have never committed adultery. I stand for integrity and conduct myself accordingly. I'm not aware of having abused or manipulated anyone in the church I pastor. Never have I deliberately wounded anyone. Nevertheless, God has used pressure in the form of accusations leveled at me for things I never thought, said, or did. There have been criticisms, abandonments, and betrayals that have exposed dark places in my character. I've been made to face and deal with a hidden need for recognition, tinges of selfish ambition, and roots of depression and discouragement that sometimes leaked out and pulled others down. Pressures, no matter how unfair, revealed blockages between God and me in the form of ungodly beliefs about Him and even about myself.

I found myself broken and weak—and that was a good thing. I honestly no longer care about being well-known, or standing on a stage in front of thousands, or being invited all over the world, or appearing on a national television show. These things mean nothing to me personally; I only want to faithfully and humbly present Jesus. Call it sanctification, if you will. This forms a platform for safely receiving the power and anointing God has already sent. When you've been awakened to these things, made aware of the impure and the unholy, and you come before the throne in repentance, allowing God to clean it all out, then you have a solid foundation on which to bear the weight of the glory and power God has sent.

HOW THEY REALLY PRAYED

In light of all this, I don't believe the one hundred and twenty were petitioning God during those ten days leading to Pentecost. Jesus didn't tell them to do that, and He didn't even tell them to pray. He told them to wait. Wait means be still and, and wait means to prepare. It does not mean to present an agenda to God. Pentecost was a gift. You don't beg for a gift you've already been promised that's already been shipped. You don't beg for the Christmas present you were told you'd receive when it's under the tree. You might hold it and shake it, but you wait until the time is right before you open it. God had promised the outpouring of the Spirit in power. It was on its way. There was therefore no more need to ask, but rather to wait as Jesus told the disciples to do, to prepare to receive and retain the power being sent.

Acting on what Jesus had breathed into them (John 20), I believe they spent those ten days prayerfully seeking purity and forgiving whatever needed to be forgiven. Offenses. Wounds. Judgments on one another. When you forgive, you cease to be a victim of those who have wounded or offended you. You're no longer the prisoner of something unclean and destructive, and you've taken up authority. God's nature is love, mercy, and forgiveness. He readily blesses what looks like Him.

> WHEN YOU FORGIVE, YOU CEASE TO BE A VICTIM OF THOSE WHO HAVE WOUNDED OR OFFENDED YOU.

POWER TO WITNESS

They waited, not for signs, wonders, and manifestations, although these came, but for the power to become effective witnesses for Jesus to all the nations. They waited for power to disciple nations and change the world. Actually, Jesus didn't even tell them to pray to be witnesses. He told them to wait for the promise that they would be empowered to be His witnesses, and they decided to pray while they waited.

They knew it would be costly because He had told them so.

Then they will deliver you to tribulation, and will kill you, and you will be hated by all nations because of My name. At that time many will fall away and will betray one another and hate one another. (Matthew 24:9–10)

As students of the Old Testament, the only Scriptures they knew, they also had an awareness of the promise of Isaiah 40:31:

Yet those who wait for the LORD will gain new strength; they will mount up with wings like eagles, they will run and not get tired, they will walk and not become weary.

The power they were about to receive would enable them to stand in victory and continue to bear witness under any kind of threat without loss of hope or joy.

For we do not want you to be unaware, brethren, of our affliction which came to us in Asia, that we were burdened excessively, beyond our strength, so that we despaired even of life; indeed, we had the sentence of death within ourselves so that we would not trust in ourselves, but in God who raises the dead; who delivered us from so great a peril of death, and will deliver us, He on whom we have set our hope. And He will yet deliver us. (2 Corinthians 1:8–10)

God never promised us an easy road, but He did promise strength and victory to overcome.

The outpouring of the Spirit on the day of Pentecost imparted power to express the love of Jesus in visible and tangible ways. Jesus never intended miracles merely for the sake of miracles, but rather miracles for the sake demonstrating to the world that God is loving, compassionate, and all powerful. Then and now, people need to see that the gospel is more than just words, theology, or mere ideas.

> JESUS PERFORMED MIRACLES TO DEMONSTRATE TO THE WORLD THAT GOD IS LOVING, COMPASSIONATE, AND ALL POWERFUL.

The disciples dedicated ten days of prayer not to trying to get God to do anything, but rather to positioning themselves to receive what God had already promised to send.

FOR US, THE SAME PROMISE?

Has the same promise been made to us? Yes. Peter's sermon on that incredible day of Pentecost presents us with a timeline:

> Peter said to them, "Repent, and each of you be baptized in the name of Jesus Christ for the forgiveness of your sins; and you will receive the gift of the Holy Spirit. For the promise is for you and your children and for all who are far off, as many as the Lord our God will call to Himself."
>
> (Acts 2:38–39)

The timeline for the promise has no end point or expiration date. It extends to all who come to believe through all the generations of God's people.

According to Peter, repentance forms the gateway. The same was true in Jesus's own preaching. It formed the heart of His message.

> *Now after John* [the Baptist] *had been taken into custody, Jesus came into Galilee, preaching the gospel of God, and saying, "The time is fulfilled, and the kingdom of God is at hand; repent and believe in the gospel."* (Mark 1:14–15)

So perhaps you say, "I don't get drunk, I don't do drugs, I don't smoke weed, I don't fornicate or commit adultery. Why repent? What do I have to repent of?" Let's repent of whatever in us prevents us from receiving. Let's wake from slumber, wait on the Lord as Jesus told the disciples to do, and actively prepare. Let's surrender whatever is in us that leads us to judge others, whatever separates us from those Jesus loves and keeps our hearts from the oneness Jesus prayed for and God blesses. Whatever breaks relationships must go to the cross. If there is something that causes division, count it sin and bring it before the throne of heaven. In whatever way we fail to see God as He is, count it impure and let Him give us new eyes.

The promise of power came to pass. *"When the day of Pentecost had come, they were all together in one place"* (Acts 2:1). During those ten days of devoted prayer, and in the days that followed, God answered Jesus's prayer, *"that they may all be one; even as You, Father, are in Me and I in You, that they also may be in Us, so that the world may believe that You sent Me"* (John 17:21). God has poured out His Spirit and is still doing it all these centuries later, but ongoing division acts as a barrier to what God is sending. Ten days of prayer had sufficiently removed three and a half years of judgments, offenses, and places of darkness in the hearts of the disciples so that they could receive what God had promised to send.

> GOD IS STILL POURING OUT HIS SPIRIT, BUT ONGOING DIVISION ACTS
> AS A BARRIER TO WHAT HE IS SENDING.

OUR SENSE OF ANTICIPATION

In recent years, many of us have felt a sense of anticipation. We know that God is about to do something huge and wonderful. The disciples in the upper room felt the very same thing after Jesus ascended into heaven. They understood what it meant to wait for the Lord and they knew that He didn't mean for them to do nothing. They knew not to be discouraged in the face of what must have felt like delay. They knew to prepare, to get ready, to allow the Holy Spirit to reveal, cleanse, and remove impediments that would have kept them from receiving what God was about to send.

What are we today praying for? Resolutions to problems? Cars and houses? Jobs? Even physical healing? The scriptural record doesn't present the disciples who became apostles as praying for physical healing in that time between the ascension and the power coming. They waited. They repented. They were cleansed. They came into oneness with one another. *"If you forgive the sins of any, their sins have been forgiven them; if you retain the sins of any, they have been retained"* (John 20:23).

BECOMING WITNESSES

Jesus told them they would be empowered to be His witnesses. When the power fell on them, they couldn't help but speak of what they'd received in Jesus. They couldn't stop talking about Him. When His Spirit carries us beyond preoccupation with ourselves, miracles happen and joy flows. They didn't pray for healing or deliverance. They simply did it. It flowed naturally from the power they'd been given.

I'll say it again: praying for revival is praying for a move of God, but He already promised a move of His Spirit and has already sent it. I think we've been begging for a gift that's already been given. Pure prophetic voices have been calling for repentance in these recent days because repentance prepares the vessel to contain what God has sent. The body of Christ has largely been asleep and unprepared. Scripturally speaking, spiritual slumber is a result of sin and idolatry. Repentance from these leads to awakening, while awakening leads to receiving.

> REPENTANCE FROM SIN AND IDOLATRY LEADS TO AWAKENING, WHILE AWAKENING LEADS TO RECEIVING.

The apostle Paul wrote, *"For I am conscious of nothing against myself, yet I am not by this acquitted; but the one who examines me is the Lord"* (1 Corinthians 4:4). Holy Spirit reveals. It's not that we're called to examine ourselves. We're not navel-gazing and trying to dig things up on our own. We're waiting on the Lord and allowing Holy Spirit to do the work of revealing.

Sometimes this means we must stop lifting up the shopping list of problems we want to be solved or the things we want to see happen, and we just say, "Holy Spirit, come. I want to be with You. I wait. Show me what I must see." As the psalmist prayed, *"Search me, O God, and know my heart; try me and know my anxious thoughts; and see if there be any hurtful way in me, and lead me in the everlasting way"* (Psalm 139:23–24). It's not me examining me. It's me crying for the Lord to examine me while I go about the business of life and obedience to His commands. Show me. Find the hurtful places. Let me be a solid vessel able to receive what You've already sent.

WARNING AND PROMISE

I remain convinced that although that remnant hungers for God and is alive to His reality, the vast majority of the body of Christ remains tragically sound asleep during a crucial season of lessened pressure intended to give us time to prepare for what is coming. We in the United States, for instance, live in a window of economic expansion, as well as a time when pressure on Christians is less than it has been because of an administration that favors both the church and Israel. Recently, for instance, religious freedom for Christians has been upheld in Supreme Court decisions, thanks to judges appointed by the current president. It would be much too easy to fall asleep during this season, too easy to fall into complacency. If we allow that to happen, we will find ourselves unprepared for the troubles to come.

In December 2016, God gave me a vision that told me we had four years in which to prepare, and that in middle of the fourth year, we would begin to see real trouble. If the current U.S. administration is voted out in the election cycle of that fourth year, the radical left will take control of the nation. In the name of the left's version of *justice* and *equality*, laws will be passed that Christians will be unable to obey. Freedoms will begin to vanish. The economy will enter an accelerating decline because of higher taxes and the destruction that socialism has always wrought wherever it has been tried.

> IF THE RADICAL LEFT TAKES CONTROL OF OUR NATION, THEIR VERSION OF JUSTICE AND EQUALITY WILL BRING ABOUT LAWS THAT CHRISTIANS WILL BE UNABLE TO OBEY.

Our military will be gutted in the name of peace and budgetary constraints. The *Pax Americana*—the American peace that has held the world's bad guys at bay and has fed every economy on the planet—will sputter and come to an end as the power of the United States fades. At that point, war will become inevitable and it will be the most destructive the world has ever seen.

We have yet time to pray for the Lord's hand to intervene and buy us more time beyond the window I saw in my vision. However long this window in time may last, we must prepare to shine in the darkness and walk in the most glorious days of our lives when this season of ease inevitably comes to an end.

Isaiah 60, filled with power and promise, is the word of hour for us.

> *Arise, shine; for your light has come, and the glory of the LORD has risen upon you. For behold, darkness will cover the earth and deep darkness the peoples; but the LORD will rise upon you and His glory will appear upon you. Nations will come to your light, and kings to the brightness of your rising. Lift up your eyes round about and see; they all gather together, they come to you. Your sons will come from afar, and your daughters will be carried in the arms.*
>
> (Isaiah 60:1–4)

As we shine in the darkness, wielding the power and love of God in an unprecedented outpouring of the Holy Spirit, a great harvest of souls will be won to Jesus, drawn by the brightness of our rising.

Know, however, that we're on the clock and we must make the most of the time we've been granted for preparation. We can pray for an extension of this season of grace and ease, and I believe God will grant it if we accompany our prayers with deep cries of repentance, both in our personal lives and on behalf of the church and our nation.

I exhort my fellow pastors, leaders, and prophetic voices to set aside concerns for the size of their congregations, which tend to shape and hinder our preaching of the Word. God didn't call us to build the church. He called us to make disciples. He Himself builds the church. We can prepare our people adequately only if we preach not *to* the people, but *from* the heart of God, boldly and without fear.

> WE CAN PREPARE OUR PEOPLE ADEQUATELY ONLY IF WE PREACH FROM THE HEART OF GOD, BOLDLY AND WITHOUT FEAR.

Many of us cry for revival, and I support that cry because I know what we mean. But we don't need revival—we need an awakening. We must come alive to the touch of God and sharpen our senses to the moving of His Spirit as well as to the condition of the world around us. This is a time for renewed passion in love for our Lord and for people in this dying world. It's a time for prayer on our faces and for battle on our feet.

Something wonderful, incredible, and huge is coming for the people of God, like a tsunami wave of the Spirit that will break suddenly and with force, although with gentleness and the sweetness of His overpowering love. Many of us are being prepared for it by the hand of God. Back in the Jesus Movement days of the 1970s, we used to say that some folks got "severely saved." Right now, some of us are being severely prepared. A shaking has come upon us. It can be violent and upsetting, but what settles out of it is firm and solid, a foundation ready to receive the powerful edifice God has prepared to place upon it. This is no flash-in-the-pan flare-up of revival that comes and goes. Neither is it an experience to be pursued as we run from conference to conference, following the spiritual superstar or the big name. This is the real thing, the Spirit descending and remaining.

13

PREPARATORY SHAKINGS TO COME

TRANSITIONS IN LEADERSHIP

Many years ago, the Lord told me that, for me, self-promotion is illegal. Ever since then, I've wrestled with the implications of that word. For the sake of profitability for the publishers who produce my books, I'm required to do some promotion of my own, but there are limits. In light of this, I've pondered what the apostle Paul had to say in Philippians 3:8 when he spoke of all that he had given up. He wrote:

> More than that, I count all things to be loss in view of the surpassing value of knowing Christ Jesus my Lord, for whom I have suffered the loss of all things, and count them but rubbish so that I may gain Christ.

"*Rubbish*" in the original Greek is actually a rather strong profanity that illustrates the depth of what the apostle wanted to communicate about the wonder of truly knowing and experiencing Jesus. For this, Paul would pay any price.

After suffering some very painful losses of my own, and considering God's prohibition against self-promotion, I've come to a conclusion similar to Paul's own understanding. For me, it takes the form of a question. How many of us in Christian leadership are focused on building our careers at the expense of a focus on intimacy with our Lord? Subtle seduction has always been a key tactic of the enemy of our soul, so that we often don't see what has happened until the damage has already been done.

> SUBTLE SEDUCTION HAS ALWAYS BEEN A KEY TACTIC
> OF THE ENEMY OF OUR SOUL.

How many of us raise and spend large sums of money to promote and build large ministry organizations, with all of the accompanying glitz and glamor, but fail to promote and impart a very simple focus on Jesus? How accessible to the average believer have we actually made the depth of intimacy with Jesus that we ourselves claim to enjoy? To what extent have we truly connected people to Jesus, rather than growing a personal following? How many barriers have we unwittingly erected by cultivating the star system based on the image of the spiritual hero on the platform or television screen?

And He gave some as apostles, and some as prophets, and some as evangelists, and some as pastors and teachers, for the equipping of the saints for the work of service, to the building up of the body of Christ.   (Ephesians 4:11–12)

We have been charged with enabling the saints to minister, perform miracles, and win the lost, not to do it *for* them.

God released the Toronto Blessing in 1994. The following year, I knew that it was such a historic outpouring that I had to see it in person. Subsequently, I became a part of the International Input Council for the church affiliation that grew out of that revival and served in that capacity for fourteen years. I knew the Toronto Blessing from the inside out.

> IN THOSE EARLY DAYS, THERE WERE NO SUPERSTARS OR BIG NAMES, BUT MANIFESTATIONS WERE EVERYWHERE.

Although it got much better as time went on, in the beginning, I found the preaching to be mediocre. Worship came through a scratchy sound system that irritated my ears as a professional musician, and it usually wasn't all that great in terms of performance. In those early days, there were no superstars or big names. It was just a lot of unknown, but faithful servants and nameless saints, ministering to one another. They were trained in a ministry team course, certainly, but were ordinary folk nevertheless. Manifestations were everywhere. People were powerfully touched, many of them laid out on the floor, unable to move for hours at a time.

People came from all over the world, not because of who the speaker would be, but because what was happening there was clearly God. None of the usual flashy and polished presentations were in evidence in those wonderful early days. It was just God—and lives were changed.

But then something began to shift. Where once it had been the simple overwhelming power of God that drew people, the attraction for too many became the name of the superstar listed in the brochure or on the website. People came because the famous name drew them. These well-known leaders are wonderful people. I respect and love them all for the magnificent gifts they have given to the body of Christ. I'm not addressing anything they've done, but rather what the body of Christ has done *to* them.

As the shift began to happen, instead of connecting with one another in mutual ministry as the body of Christ is called to do, meetings and conferences seemed to become more centered on expecting the superstar on the platform to do it for them. As this developed, it seemed to me that the anointing began to fade. We began to lose a measure of the wonder of what God was doing sovereignly. Others might have a different point of view, but this was my experience.

THE LORD GIVES A VISION AND A WORD

Years later, in early 2019, the Lord gave me a vision of the hand of God grasping the trunk of a tree and shaking it powerfully until a rain of debris began to fall from it. The Lord Himself interpreted the vision:

> The day is coming when I will shake out the dead limbs and the dried fruit, leaders who lead where I have not led and prophets who speak the profane, watered-down messages of peace when there is no peace. I have hovered over My people lightly. I am about to descend in storm and great shaking. Some will fall. Others will rise. Some who were unknown are about to be known. I am making a tall tower to proclaim My truth. All men will see and be vexed at My outpouring of grace and love. You will be surprised at the fall of many, but I have preserved My servants for such a day as this, a day of release, a day of mercy. Where mercy exists, the power will fall and My name will be known. The leadership tree is Mine to

prune and a pruning is about to unfold, not in judgment, but for increase. Some have already faded away, but I am bringing more. More will fade away and more will come, rising in the brightness of My shining.

My sense of what happened to the revival movement that began in the 1990s, together with the vision I received in 2019, points to a great shift in the body of Christ. We are about to see a shaking out of the tree of leadership and a restoration of the ministry of the body of Christ in fullness. This shaking began with the worldwide coronavirus crisis and will continue in the days to come.

> **GREAT MINISTRIES THAT HAVE GARNERED ATTENTION, BUT FAILED IN HUMBLE FOCUS ON THE HEART OF JESUS, WILL FALL.**

Great ministries that have garnered the attention of the church and the world, but failed in humble focus on the heart of Jesus, or failed to truly equip the saints, will fall. In their place, we'll see a new breed of leadership emerge, immersed in the Father's love, obsessed with Jesus, and dedicated to releasing and unleashing the power of the Holy Spirit in every believer. This new breed won't seek or care for the spotlight or the stage, but God will place them in the spotlight and stand them on prominent platforms precisely because they don't seek nor need these things for themselves.

In Matthew 19:12, Jesus made a troubling statement:

For there are eunuchs who were born that way from their mother's womb; and there are eunuchs who were made eunuchs by men; and there are also eunuchs who made themselves eunuchs for the sake of the kingdom of heaven. He who is able to accept this, let him accept it.

Ancient kings employed eunuchs to guard their harems because eunuchs would be immune to temptation to attract the attention of the king's women to themselves or to violate them in any way. They would guard the harem and keep it pure for the sake of the king. God seeks spiritual eunuchs in our day who will care for the bride of Christ for the sake of the King of Kings, our bridegroom, without being tempted to sample her affections for themselves. God has been shaking that which can be shaken in order to bring about that kind of purity.

In the same way that the apostle Paul suffered the loss of all things for the sake of knowing Jesus and sharing in everything that Jesus is, God seeks for humble and broken servants and mouthpieces who have nothing left to lose and cannot, therefore, be tempted. They'll be given great ministries with broad impact precisely because they don't need great ministries with broad impact. Their singular desire will be to see the name of Jesus lifted up rather than their own. Their goal will be to see the bride of Christ in love with Him. These will deliver a pure word. God Himself will be their promoter. Our Lord is looking for friends, not handlers, the genuine rather than the show, and the heart rather than the performance.

> OUR LORD IS LOOKING FOR THE GENUINE RATHER THAN THE SHOW, THE HEART RATHER THAN THE PERFORMANCE.

THE COMING PROPHETIC SHIFT

In 2011, I wrote the following in *Visions of the Coming Days*:

A new generation of leadership is emerging to lead a fresh generation of the body of Christ who will shine with His nature. Signs and wonders, power ministry, and healing will follow after those the Lord reveals as those who have come to look like Him, carrying the Father's heart, but the focus of their lives will not fall on the supernatural. Real holiness and genuine supernatural power flow inside out from godly wholeness that results in the kind of intimacy with God that Jesus spoke of when He said that He and the Father were one. Inner change produces outward action and consistently good fruit.[3]

One outcome of the coronavirus crisis is that God has accelerated a shift in the prophetic world. A cleansing of much that has been impure has been underway. For many years, we have seen too many prophetic words fail the test of fulfillment. Purification has become an urgent issue. As this gathers steam in the days to come, it will also include a changing of the guard. While faithful patriarchs such as John Paul Jackson, Bishop Bill Haman, and my own father, John Sandford, to name a few, paved the way for reliable prophetic ministry, it seems clear that a fresh set of voices will now carry it forward. An older generation is passing away or simply fading from the spotlight while a fresh group of anointed prophets is just beginning to emerge.

> MORE THAN DEVELOPING THEIR GIFTS, THE EMERGING GENERATION WILL SEEK ONENESS WITH JESUS AND HIS NATURE.

While I am not saying there was anything less than godliness in those now fading from the spotlight or in those now gone home to glory—and while I am certainly not in any way minimizing the contributions they made to the body of Christ—I *am* saying that the emerging generation carries a fresh heart for a new day. These will speak more from humble intimacy with

---

3. R. Loren Sandford, *Visions of the Coming Days: What to Look for and How to Prepare* (Bloomington, MN: Chosen Books, 2012).

Jesus and from a pastoral spirit than from a concern for gifting. Their words will flow more from the heart of the Father than from any felt need to prophesy, build a great ministry, or stand on anyone's stage. More than developing their gifts, they will seek oneness with Jesus and His nature. They will pursue rest in relationship with Him, more than being supernatural.

The aforementioned pioneers pointed the way with an emphasis on character, the cross, and biblical grounding, but in my opinion, their foundational core messages were too little heard by too many who needed to listen. In this coming generation, however, the call to integrity, character, and solid biblical grounding will be heeded. More than developing their gifts, they will seek oneness with Jesus and His nature, pursuing rest in relationship with Jesus more than being supernatural. The need to wow the body of Christ and tickle the ears of men will give way to a hunger to bow before the King of Kings, broken by His love and faithful to His words, regardless of the fallout. As a result, these emerging prophets will release into the people of God a deeper level of life than we have known, as well as a sense of liberty in holiness that is both life-giving and free of condemnation.

FATHERING THE COMING PROPHETIC GENERATION

We older ones whom God allows to remain—some of us perhaps late maturers in matters prophetic, hidden by the hand of God until now—inherit a calling to father the coming movement. The heart of a true father desires to see sons and daughters grow into greater things than he could ever attain. Those into whom we sow life and wisdom may therefore carry greater gifting and walk in a higher level of revelation than we who are called to be fathers have known, but so did Elisha exercise a greater level of raw anointing than did his spiritual father, Elijah.

What if those in this emerging generation become better known than those of us called to father them? What if their books sell more than ours? What if they stand before thousands as we merely watch and pray? Can we walk in the kind of humility that rejoices to see others gaining notice and recognition for their full-grown wisdom and the revelations for which we sowed the seeds in hidden places? Will our hearts swell with pleasure and pride in their advancement? Or will old wineskins and unredeemed elements of character, ambition, and insecurity disqualify us and hinder us from delivering and releasing the fullness of the treasure God has entrusted to us for their sake?

WHAT WILL HAPPEN WHEN THESE YOUNGER VOICES CONFRONT ABUSES AND IMBALANCES IN PROPHETIC MINISTRIES?

When these younger voices confront abuses and imbalances in prophetic ministries, will an older, more established prophetic community receive and judge their words on the basis of the humble spirit in which they are delivered and the soundness of their biblical grounding? Or will there be rejection and backlash with cries of, "Who does that young guy think he is, correcting and rebuking major internationally known ministries?!"

The apostle Paul exhorted young Timothy not to allow anyone to look down on him for his youth, but rather to exercise the gifting, anointing, and authority imparted to him through the laying on of Paul's hands. Will an older generation need to be exhorted regarding the flip side of Paul's admonition so that, in fact, the older generation does not despise the younger for being what I might call *chronologically handicapped*?

GOING LOWER TO RISE HIGHER

Paradoxically, the higher calling carries us to lower places. In the economy of God, we rise above by coming under. We become the first by becoming the last. By serving, we rule and reign while we store up an eternal reward in heaven that never fades or dies away.

Over the years, it has often been said that one cannot be both pastor and prophet, as if the two were opposed to one another. While that might once have seemed true, part of the coming shift involves the emergence of pastor/prophets and prophet/pastors. The days are passing when prophetic ministries can stand alone, outside the local church. God calls prophets to be integral parts of the local church, submitted to its disciplines and committed to its people, pregnant with their life as the apostle Paul was pregnant with the life of the church in Galatia. (See Galatians 4:19.) The prophet/pastor and pastor/prophet speak from the inside out, not from the outside in. He or she stands in and under, not apart from the local church.

The shift underway in the prophetic world has only just begun and was accelerated by the coronavirus crisis. It will unfold in two waves over time: 1) the passing or retirement of an older generation and the emergence of a fresh and mostly younger one; and 2) a cleansing of prophetic ministry to discredit and eliminate pollutions and abuses across a broad front. We need, and we will have, a more accurate flow of prophetic ministry in the body of Christ, faithful to the Father's heart in Jesus. God our Father will see to it for the vindication of His own name.

PROPHETIC DISILLUSIONMENT

In my travels and online, I encounter increasing numbers of people disillusioned with the prophetic movement. There have been too many unfulfilled prophecies, dates set and missed, catastrophic events that never happened, promises that didn't unfold, moral failings on the part of some prophetic leaders, and a growing number of biblical imbalances and outright heresies. Too much of the prophetic movement has gotten it wrong or wandered off base. Remember the Y2K (year 2000) prophecies that never happened? Or the prophetic words that said the coronavirus would end suddenly during Passover? Credibility has been eroded. All of this takes an increasing toll on confidence in the prophetic gift, and it has led some to begin to think that the prophetic gift is not for today.

Consider, however, 1 Kings 22, when kings Jehoshaphat and Ahab sought the will of the Lord on whether to engage in battle to retake Ramoth-Gilead from Aram. They called a convention of four hundred prophets, who then read the desire in the kings' hearts, listened to a deceiving spirit (see verses 22:22–23), and told Jehoshaphat and Ahab what they wanted to hear: "Go up to Ramoth-Gilead and prosper, for the Lord will give it into the hand of the king."

In his spirit, Micaiah alone knew the truth, but initially spoke in unison with the four hundred. Only when Ahab commanded him to do so did he relent and speak what he really knew:

> I saw all Israel scattered on the mountains, like sheep which have no shepherd. And the LORD said, "These have no master. Let each of them return to his house in peace."... Therefore, hear the word of the LORD. I saw the LORD sitting on His throne, and all the host of heaven standing by Him on His right and on His left. The LORD said, "Who will entice Ahab to go up and fall at Ramoth-gilead?" And one said this while another said that. Then a spirit came

forward and stood before the LORD *and said, "I will entice him."*   (1 Kings 22:17, 19–21)

Apparently, a prophetic movement was underway in Israel such that four hundred so-called prophets could hold a convention. Who in that day who truly heard God's voice would have had the faith, the courage, and the confidence to disagree with the dominant stream, especially with a word that didn't sound particularly encouraging? Truth comes with a price! Micaiah stood alone against two kings and four hundred acclaimed prophetic voices, only to suffer humiliation when Zedekiah, one of the false prophets' leaders, slapped his face for not joining with the majority. (See 1 Kings 22:24.) Micaiah then found himself imprisoned and fed sparingly on bread and water. (See verse 27.)

Ultimately, four hundred "prophets" had it wrong, Israel suffered defeat, and Ahab was killed. Regardless of consequences to Ahab and the army because of the inaccurate words of the four hundred, Israel did not scuttle prophecy as a ministry. Prophetic failure on the part of the majority did not lead them to declare all prophetic ministry invalid. Rather, because one prophet had it right, prophecy continued to be seen as a valid ministry both in Israel and, later, in the church. It would seem that the key lies not in how many are speaking a particular word, but in discernment to know who actually speaks from God's heart.

Do we have a dearth of real discernment in the church today? Are we too ready to hear only what excites us and what we want to hear? Have we relegated true prophetic voices, ever the minority, to the sidelines and locked them up because they don't go with the dominant flow?

REPEATEDLY THROUGHOUT HISTORY, THERE HAVE BEEN OCCASIONS AND SEASONS WHEN THE TRUTH HAS RESTED WITH THE LESS POPULAR MINORITY.

Repeatedly throughout history, there have been occasions and seasons when the truth has rested not with the dominant word being spoken by the majority, but with the less popular minority. Sometimes, they do not become respected or well-known until after their deaths. They threw Jeremiah down a well and disregarded his words. Elijah was called the troubler of Israel. And so it went!

Maybe we need to stop listening so intently to the popular voices who speak with the mainstream and whose words we love to hear. Could it be that a purified remnant speaks a plumb-line word that doesn't win them the platform of widespread popularity? Can we discern the word of God in a hidden but emerging generation of prophetic voices who might not speak what we *want* to hear, but who certainly speak what we *need* to hear? In doing so, might we be more edified and more prepared for the glory to come in the midst of a gathering darkness?

CROSSING THE LINE PROPHETICALLY

Certain boundaries and disciplines must be heeded and practiced. Prophetic ministry must never be taken lightly or too easily franchised. Mature prophets understand that some lines must never be crossed.

WHEN YOU HAVE NOTHING TO SAY

When people see you as a prophet but you have nothing to prophesy, what do you feel? The answer is that you sense the expectations and demands of the people for you to deliver words from God. You have meetings to lead, articles to write, and questions to answer, and so you pray. You worship. You fellowship with God and you sense His presence, but maybe you find yourself stuck in a season or a setting in which the words just don't come. You might worry that you've somehow lost your anointing or that the gift has died. But that's not possible, is it? The gifts and the calling of God are irrevocable, according to Scripture, right? What to do?

At that point, you need to rest in the knowledge that faithful and true prophets never prophesy merely because they're prophetic or because they can. They prophesy when God is speaking and *only* when God is speaking. Never is the true prophetic word under the control or command of the prophet. You might point to 1 Corinthians 14:32, *"And the spirits of prophets are subject to prophets,"* but the language is that their *"spirits"* are under control. The inner urge, character, and drive of the prophet are subject to the prophet, but the word itself is not. The word itself must be the Lord's. If the prophetic word were under control of the prophet, then it would no longer be the word of the Lord, but rather something from the mind, heart, and imagination of the speaker. One of the most difficult lessons for any so-called prophet to learn is to keep quiet when God falls silent, even when the season of silence seems to be endless.

> ONE OF THE MOST DIFFICULT LESSONS FOR ANY SO-CALLED PROPHET TO LEARN IS TO KEEP QUIET WHEN GOD FALLS SILENT.

What happens when that line has been crossed? We get four hundred prophets speaking from a deceiving spirit into the desires of the kings, while just one, Micaiah, gets it right. The kings then choose to follow after the positive words of the majority who bring the popular word, ignoring the warning delivered by the one. Israel loses. King Ahab dies. (See 1 Kings 22.)

You get Hananiah prophesying Israel's deliverance from Babylon's domination while Jeremiah tells the truth that he himself wants neither to hear nor speak. Guess which prophetic voice the people responded to? Hananiah died while Babylon intensified their conquest of Israel. Israel spent seventy years in exile. (Read Jeremiah 28 and more.)

UNFULFILLED WORDS

Many times in my travels, I've asked an audience how many have received prophecies that never came to pass. Often, more than half the hands in the room spring up from people with hurt and disillusionment in their eyes. How many prophecies spoken over your church, your nation, or the world have simply failed to come to pass?

Could it be that too many prophetic ministers and prophetic ministries have responded to the pressure of the people, the need to crank out words that fund the ministry and feed their own need to shine? Could it be that, as a result, they prophesy from their own hearts without even realizing they are doing so? Could it be that they speak in the Lord's name, not because they have actually heard from God, but because both they and the people see them as prophetic? Could it be that they speak from their gifting, or from the flesh parading itself in supernatural clothing, rather than from intimacy with God?

I myself often feel these same pressures in the course of my own ministry, both in my local congregation and when I travel to minister in other places. Have I mastered the discernment needed to know the difference between prophesying merely because I'm prophetic, and prophesying because God is truly speaking? No, I haven't, but I understand the quest, and I want to cultivate the courage and integrity to resist the pressures. If this results in extended seasons when I feel rather ordinary, so be it. Representing God accurately must take precedence over any form of fame, personal recognition, or sense of personal significance and authority. More importantly, what comes from my mouth must never be a reflection of what people want to hear, but rather what God wants to say.

> REPRESENTING GOD ACCURATELY MUST TAKE PRECEDENCE OVER ANY FAME, RECOGNITION, OR SENSE OF PERSONAL SIGNIFICANCE AND AUTHORITY.

Don't we all owe this both to God and to His people? Shouldn't we as the body of Christ be holding our contemporary prophets accountable for what they present in the name of the Lord? I am deeply concerned that we need to take prophesying much more seriously than we seem to be taking it in many quarters today. *"You shall not take the name of the LORD your God in vain"* (Exodus 20:7) means precisely that you must not claim that your words are the Lord's words if they are not truly His words.

PROPHETIC REFORMATION

For the sake of God's people and the world, we *must* do better than we have done! Here are five elements essential to prophetic accuracy and integrity. Let's repair the damage before too many more people reject both the gift and, ultimately, the One who gives it.

1. CHARACTER

No one will ever prophesy accurately through the filter of a broken core character. Broken character produces broken words, just as a bad lens distorts vision. No prophetic word will ever be the real thing apart from the heart and nature of the Father imparted into us. The words themselves might be accurate, but if the spirit in which those words are delivered fails to communicate the heart of God, whose nature is love, then it will not be the word of God. Absent a wilderness experience for the shaping and refining of character, such so-called prophets will be loose cannons on the Lord's deck, dangerous to others and even to themselves.

My son once said that we are looking for *kingdom people* to hold leadership positions in our church. He defined such people as those who are changing and being changed. He's right. Are we embracing the Father's heart, gazing so deeply into the face of Jesus that we are being transformed into His image? How willing are we to confront those parts of ourselves that have yet to be redeemed, or to embrace the pressure and pain sent to reveal those flaws? My own prayer is that He will let me have His heart, His humility, and His grace so that I might accurately and fully speak in His name.

2. SOLID BIBLICAL GROUNDING

Personal revelation must never be allowed to trump the eternal Word of God, once received and never changing. Prophetic words may be sparked by spiritual inspiration, but they must flow from and through Scripture, tested, bound, and refined by eternal truth. Over the years, we have suffered an avalanche of unfulfilled prophetic words that have served to discredit prophetic ministry, not only in the eyes of much of the church, but in the eyes of the world as well. Much of this has been the result of faulty understanding of Scripture and, in some cases, blatant contradictions of what the Scriptures actually say.

> PROPHETIC WORDS MAY BE SPARKED BY SPIRITUAL INSPIRATION, BUT THEY MUST FLOW FROM AND THROUGH SCRIPTURE.

For example, there is no such thing as "Christian" numerology or astrology. Both are mocked and condemned in multiple passages of the Bible that point us to the voice of the Lord Himself rather than to any other source. Some protest that Genesis says the lights in the heavens are given for signs and seasons, and can therefore be taken as messages from God. True. *They mark signs and seasons!* What this means is that by them, prior to the invention of mechanical clocks, mankind could mark time. By them, we would know when to plant, when to harvest, when to prepare for winter, and so on. In the same way that the hands of the mechanical clock indicate the hour, predictable, repeatable astronomical events that result from the mechanical operation of the universe mark the seasons. They were never intended, however, as special supernatural messages or warnings from God.

On the other hand, unpredictable signs in the heavens can certainly be taken as direct messages or warnings from God. The star of Bethlehem moved and stopped to indicate where the baby Jesus lay. Stars don't behave that way naturally. *That* was a sign from God, not a predictable mechanical alignment of the stars.

When understood in their biblical context, *shemitahs*, which have been written about and caused such a stir in recent years, do not predict seven-year cycles of economics, as some have proposed. Biblically speaking, in the seventh year, the fields were to lie fallow in order to rest and regenerate. To pull that out of its context and apply it to economic cycles is to impose upon the Scriptures a meaning neither intended nor implied. Thus, the prophecies associated with the seven-year *shemitah* cycle never materialized.

> WE MUST REFRAIN FROM IMPOSING OUR OWN MYSTICAL INTERPRETATIONS ON SCRIPTURES.

We must recommit ourselves to discerning the meanings intended by those who wrote the Scriptures and refrain from imposing our own mystical interpretations upon the text. The apostle Paul admonished us to learn not to exceed what is written. (See 1 Corinthians 4:6.) Should we not take that warning very seriously?

3. INTIMACY WITH THE LORD

I'm a thinking man, sometimes to a fault and sometimes at the expense of sensing the Lord experientially, although this is changing for the better as I grow older, grayer, and softer. Balance is coming. In conjunction with reason, therefore, I weigh and think through my spiritual senses. I desire never to allow the reasoning part of my nature to prevent me from experiencing the Lord and allowing His heart to inform my understanding. While I will never make a quest of seeking to be supernatural, I will passionately seek intimacy with the Three, Father, Son and Holy Spirit, knowing that this will make me supernatural. Those who focus on being supernatural will end up in shipwreck and delusion. Those who focus on intimacy with God will find themselves being solidly and reliably supernatural.

> THOSE WHO FOCUS ON BEING SUPERNATURAL WILL END UP IN SHIPWRECK AND DELUSION.

4. CHECKS AND BALANCES

I believe the days are coming to an end when prophetic ministries can operate independently outside the checks and balances of the local church. We must establish structures in the body of Christ for testing both the character of the prophetic speaker and the content of the words spoken. In the context of the public worship service, the apostle Paul expressed a principle for local church checks and balances that I believe actually goes beyond the confines of the public gathering: *"Let two or three prophets speak, and let the others pass judgment"* (1 Corinthians 14:29).

In other words, every prophetic person needs relationships with people who speak truth and enforce balance, testing what comes from the prophetic speaker. Prophetic ministry thrives on healthy relationships. These relationships must not be made up of mere followers and admirers, but people who, while respecting the gift and the office, nevertheless see the humanity of the prophet and speak fearlessly into it with love.

Iron sharpens iron, so one man sharpens another.
(Proverbs 27:17)

Faithful are the wounds of a friend, but deceitful are the kisses of an enemy.
(Proverbs 27:6)

5. HUMILITY AND BROKENNESS

Does the following reflect your experience? When was the last time you heard a prophetic person admit to being wrong when prophecies you heard or received didn't pan out? When was the last time you heard a public apology when a well-publicized prophetic word failed to come to pass? Such confessions happen, but in my experience only rarely. In the year 2000, after so many prophetic voices missed it with the Y2K prophecies of disaster, how many open apologies did you hear? When prophecies related to the coronavirus crisis didn't quite pan out, were there public confessions? When words spoken by a prophetic voice over your personal life or ministry failed to come to pass, how many of us were approached by that same prophetic person expressing sorrow and seeking to make amends? How many such prophets even take time to follow up to check on their accuracy?

Have we become too full of ourselves and overly impressed with the gifts in which we move, or do we walk in the kind of humility that recognizes those gifts belong to Him, not to us, and that, if He felt it to be necessary, He could withdraw the anointing in a heartbeat? Do we respond to criticism with grace and mercy, or with anger and defense?

TWO RULES OF MINISTRY

I have a list of rules of ministry I seek to live by. Here are two of them:

1. Never believe your own press.

2. Success is always, and in every case, toxic.

Don't be put off by number two. God wants us to succeed. He gets no glory and takes no pleasure in our failures. Just understand that the most dangerous time in any leader's walk is the point at which success comes. It's all too easy to transition from being full of the Spirit to being full of ourselves. The rush we experience in the glow of success and the adulation people shower upon us can lead us to fail to recognize the moment of transition from Spirit to flesh. All of us need people in our lives who remind us how wonderful we are, but these must also be free to say, "You suck" when we need to hear it. We desperately need a prophetic reformation for our generation. Let it begin now and let it begin with us.

14

A CULTURE OF COVENANT

Every nation or people that has ever existed has had a culture of customs, traditions, and ways of thinking and doing things that carry meaning and power to shape entire people groups. As you were raised in the culture, so you learned. The whole of Scripture is steeped in the culture of the people who lived when those Bible stories, events, and revelations unfolded. God loves culture. In the Bible, He spoke through culture, using cultural language and symbols its people understood.

Some of that culture is 4,000 years old and no longer exists. As a result, we have tended to miss the heart of what God was doing and saying, but the meaning of what He did so long ago remains. The ways and customs of the culture of biblical times died out thousands of years ago, but the truth God communicated through it stands for eternity.

THE MISSING FOUNDATION

I hear a lot of culture talk in the church today, a lot of language tossed around that, while it may be true, tends to lose its meaning because it misses an essential foundation, the truth that's embedded in the most ancient cultural traditions and ceremonies of the Bible. The foundational issue of culture I raise here is a phrase I've not heard anywhere else. We need a *culture of covenant* to undergird what God wants to pour out in these last days.

> **WE NEED A CULTURE OF COVENANT TO UNDERGIRD WHAT GOD WANTS TO POUR OUT IN THESE LAST DAYS.**

In ancient Bible times, there were procedures and traditions involved in establishing a covenant that have been lost to us. In Genesis 15, God had already reached out to Abraham, called him to leave his father's country, and go to a new land. He'd already chosen and prospered him, but the covenant God was about to make was a whole lot more than any of that.

For Abraham, whose name was still Abram, it was time for a step-up, for a destiny of blessing and favor to be truly launched, and so God came to Abram, not yet Abraham, in a vision and began to make promises. God was about to establish a covenant with Abraham and that began, as all covenants did, with promises and commitments. God said, *"I am a shield to you; your reward shall be very great"* (Genesis 15:1). Abram's reply was, *"What will You give me, since I am childless?"* (verse 2). In other words, how could all this be when a man who had no child was considered cursed for lack of a posterity?

In Genesis 15:4, God promised a son, something of vital importance to a man in ancient times, and then said, *"Now look toward the heavens, and count the stars, if you are able to count them....So shall your descendants be*" (verse 5). God expanded the promise by committing to give land to Abraham (verse 7), who wondered, "*O Lord GOD, how may I know that I will possess it?*" (Genesis 15:8).

> ## BLOOD COVENANT IS THE THREAD HOLDING THE WHOLE BIBLE TOGETHER.

In response, God *cut a covenant* with Abraham—very specific language because animals were cut and blood was shed. God established a blood covenant with Abraham. Blood covenant is the thread holding the whole Bible together, both Old and New Testaments. It stands at the heart of the story of salvation. Blood covenant would bestow blessings, rights, and privileges, but it also came with obligations and penalties if it was violated or broken.

The parties to the establishment of a blood covenant observed certain ceremonies and procedures. The first step in establishing a blood covenant was that one person had to initiate it by asking for it. Abraham asked God for a firm and clear guarantee that God would do what He promised! God responded by initiating the ceremony of what we might call the blood brother covenant:

> So He said to him, "*Bring Me a three year old heifer, and a three year old female goat, and a three year old ram, and a turtledove, and a young pigeon.*" *Then he brought all these to Him and cut them in two, and laid each half opposite the other; but he did not cut the birds.*   (Genesis 15:9–10)

Abram, not yet renamed Abraham, cut the animals in two because entering a blood covenant constituted a promise unto death for each partner to the covenant, symbolized by the sacrifice of the animals. This was a way of calling death on the one who would violate the covenant. Partners to the covenant would each make promises, commitments to their common life, pointing to the sacrificed animals and saying, "May God do so to me and more if I ever break or violate the covenant we make today."

Blood covenant bound the lives of the participants together in an exchange of life, one life for the other life, as if to say, "Now whatever I have is at your disposal and whatever you have is at my disposal. We are bound now as family to one another." To symbolize this exchange, they would each pass between the two halves of the animal, passing one another in a figure eight, changing places. In the covenant with Abraham, God Himself passed between the pieces of the sacrificial animals.

> *It came about when the sun had set, that it was very dark, and behold, there appeared a smoking oven and a flaming torch which passed between these pieces. On that day the LORD made a covenant with Abram, saying, "To your descendants I have given this land."* (Genesis 15:17–18)

In this covenant, God promised a son to Abraham, countless descendants, and land for them to occupy. But it goes farther even than that. Blood covenants were made with blessings and curses. In the blessing, each partner to the covenant had access to all the assets of the other whenever needed. If one encountered trouble, the other would be there and have his back. They would stand together in the face of all things. This was the blessing.

To fail in that commitment and violate the covenant was to bring down a curse. An example is found much later in Jeremiah 34, where the kings and rulers in Judah had been disobedient to a clear command of the Lord to set their servants free in the seventh year of their servitude. They had violated a covenant they had made with God by passing between the cut halves of a sacrificial animal. God responded with the curse:

> *I will give the men who have transgressed My covenant, who have not fulfilled the words of the covenant which they made before Me, when they cut the calf in two and passed between its parts—the officials of Judah and the officials of Jerusalem, the court officers and the priests and all the people of the land who passed between the parts of the calf—I will give them into the hand of their enemies and into the hand of those who seek their life. And their dead bodies will be food for the birds of the sky and the beasts of the earth.* (Jeremiah 34:18–20)

Blood covenant carries with it certain obligations on the part of both parties. Blessing comes with fulfilling covenant obligations. Failure to fulfill those obligations brings down the curse: defeat before enemies, inability to overcome obstacles.

Blood covenant involved an exchange of weapons and a promise that if one party faced an enemy or suffered an injustice, that party had the right to call on the full resources of his blood covenant partner for help and that partner would come.

> **GOD HAS BOUND HIMSELF TO US IN BLOOD COVENANT, FIRST THROUGH ABRAHAM AND THEN BY THE BLOOD OF JESUS.**

We must understand that God has bound Himself to us in blood covenant, first through Abraham and then by the blood of Jesus. The covenant with Abraham was a blood covenant. The blood of Jesus is likewise a blood covenant through the body of Jesus slain for us. He *will* come. He *will* defend us. He is our mighty fortress, our deliverer. This is all covenant language.

When we receive the blood covenant in Jesus, all that is God's is ours and all that is ours is God's. Under blood covenant, we have the covenant right to petition heaven for justice, for God to come our aid, and to access the full might of our Lord against any enemy who unjustly opposes us. But *we* are also under obligation to defend Him, to stand for Him, and to give all that we have for Him.

BLOOD COVENANT EXTENDED

The covenant reaches beyond just that which binds God to us and us to God as individuals. When we become part of the body of Christ, we become party to the covenant He cut with His people. The terms of the blood covenant become binding upon us in our relationships with one another. In his second letter to Timothy, the apostle Paul made a long list of covenant violations:

> *For men will be lovers of self, lovers of money, boastful, arrogant, revilers, disobedient to parents, ungrateful, unholy, unloving, irreconcilable, malicious gossips, without self-control, brutal, haters of good, treacherous, reckless, conceited, lovers of pleasure rather than lovers of God, holding to a form of godliness, although they have denied its power.*
> (2 Timothy 3:2–5)

This list represents elements opposed to the promises made in a blood covenant after the biblical model. When we break our covenant with one another, we violate the blood covenant with God. In doing so, we forfeit covenant protections in these last days and the penalty is, "*They have denied its power.*" Think miracles diminished as power is denied or cut off. Think fewer lives changed. Struggles will be more difficult when facing obstacles. There will be a loss of joy.

In the blood brother covenant, there was a name change, as each party adopted the other as family. You therefore took on a part of your covenant partner's name while your partner took part of yours. In Genesis 17:5, Abram's name was changed to Abraham, inserting one syllable of God's name, Yah. In the same way, his wife Sarai becomes Sarah. (See Genesis 17:15.) We take a part of Jesus's own name, Messiah, when we use the name *Christian*, which comes from the Greek translation of Messiah: *Christos*. We've taken His name, a new identity.

Every blood covenant ended with a covenant meal to celebrate the union and the promises that formed the centerpiece of the covenant. Blood covenant unites the whole Bible and bonds the people of God to one another in love. We celebrate this covenant with Communion, Eucharist, or the Last Supper, depending on religious background and practice. In the Communion service, as we dedicate the elements of Communion, we quote Jesus as He spoke in ancient covenant language:

> *And when He had taken a cup and given thanks, He gave it to them, saying, "Drink from it, all of you; for this is My blood of the covenant."* (Matthew 26:27–28)

> *And in the same way He took the cup after they had eaten, saying, "This cup which is poured out for you is the new covenant in My blood."* (Luke 22:20)

Every time we celebrate Communion, we participate in a covenant meal in which we declare and affirm that we have a blood covenant with God and with one another. It should be a time for reaffirming our promises and oaths before Him as well as remembering His promises and oaths to us. It should be a time of remembering how the covenant bonds us with one another.

This explains the apostle Paul's upset with the Corinthian church over the manner in which they celebrated Communion:

> *I do not praise you, because you come together not for the better but for the worse. For, in the first place, when you come together as a church, I hear that divisions exist among you; and in part I believe it. For there must also be factions among you, so that those who are approved may become evident among you. Therefore when you meet together, it is not to eat the Lord's Supper, for in your eating each one takes his own supper first; and one is hungry and another is drunk.* (1 Corinthians 11:17–21)

In their celebration of the covenant, they violated its terms by failing in relationship.

A CULTURE OF COVENANT TODAY

All of this brings me to this point. I hear a lot of talk in the body of Christ today about a culture of honor in which we build one another up and honor even those who have behaved dishonorably. I've seen it work for a while and then I've seen it fail because the essential foundation for a culture of honor too often is missing. It seems that sometimes, the worst violators are the ones who were the most enthusiastic promoters of it. A culture of honor must be built upon a foundation of a culture of covenant connection and mutual sacrifice, or it will fail. We have become parties to a covenant made and built upon biblical terms.

> A CULTURE OF HONOR MUST BE BUILT UPON A FOUNDATION OF A CULTURE OF COVENANT CONNECTION AND MUTUAL SACRIFICE, OR IT WILL FAIL.

For many years, we've talked and taught the Father's heart and sought a culture of the Father's heart in the church, but after a while, it always seems to devolve into just a set of words we repeat because it's missing the essential foundation found in that ancient culture from the Bible. The Father's heart *is* a heart of covenant. He's a covenant God who calls us to practice that covenant among ourselves in Him. Because He's a covenant God, Jesus said, "I will never leave you nor forsake you." (See, for example, Matthew 28:20; John 14:18; Hebrews 13:5.) This kind of commitment is included in the blood covenant bond. He bound Himself to us, but blood covenant commitments are always two-sided. *Both* parties are bound. We who are *in Christ* have been called into a bond *with one another* in the same way for the simple reason that Jesus cut the covenant with us. If we are truly *in* Him, then His blood covenant commitments become ours as well.

Blood covenant is the thread that binds most of the New Testament together and makes it one word with one message carried forward from the Old Testament. Hear the covenant language in Jesus's prayer in John 17. His covenant commitments become ours.

> *I do not ask on behalf of these alone, but for those also who believe in Me through their word; that they may all be one; even as You, Father, are in Me and I in You, that they also may be in Us, so that the world may believe that You sent Me. The glory which You have given Me I have given to them, **that they may be one**, just as We are one; I in them and You in Me, that they may be perfected in unity, so that the world may know that You sent Me, and loved them, even as You have loved Me.*   (John 17:20–23)

Similarly, Philippians 2 contains the language of blood covenant obligations.

Do nothing from selfishness or empty conceit, but with humility of mind regard one another as more important than yourselves; do not merely look out for your own personal interests, but also for the interests of others. Have this attitude in yourselves which was also in Christ Jesus.

(Philippians 2:3–5)

Remember the exchange of life, your life is now my life? The exchange of weapons for mutual defense? Your family is now my family? I don't believe we will ever see a lasting revival, the end-time outpouring of the Holy Spirit, until and unless we develop a culture of covenant to undergird it.

THE CULTURE OF COVENANT DEFINED

I'm speaking of an atmosphere of attitude, practice, and commitment to one another in the body of Christ that teaches everyone in it to live in a sacrificial, selfless way just by being part of it. In a culture of covenant, each individual exists for the benefit of the whole, while the whole exists to benefit and strengthen the individual.

Blood covenant implies commitment to one another that cannot be broken because of our commitment to Jesus. In God's covenant with Abraham, the split animal and smoking pot meant that God would give all for Abraham and nothing would deter Him from doing so. Abraham was a failure on so many fronts. He gave his wife into a foreign king's harem to save his own skin. In a failure of faith, he fathered an illegitimate child by his wife's maid, Hagar. In the face of this, God stood by him because that's what covenant does. Even though Abraham failed, he never let go of God because that was Abraham's side of the covenant commitment. God, for His part, never let go of Abraham. Jesus gave His life for that covenant.

Do not grieve the Holy Spirit of God, by whom you were sealed for the day of redemption. Let all bitterness and wrath and anger and clamor and slander be put away from you, along with all malice. Be kind to one another, tender-hearted, forgiving each other, just as God in Christ also has forgiven you. (Ephesians 4:30–32)

This again is covenant language, the bond not broken, no matter what. It's what Jesus gave us. It's part of what He died to give us in the blood covenant cut in His broken body. It's what we give one another in a culture of covenant. There is therefore nothing we don't forgive, nothing to which we grant the power to drive us away from one another.

We see blood covenant implications in the spiritual gifts.

But to each one is given the manifestation of the Spirit for the common good…so that there may be no division in the body, but that the members may have the same care for one another. And if one member suffers, all the members suffer with it; if one member is honored, all the members rejoice with it. Now you are Christ's body, and individually members of it. (1 Corinthians 12:7, 25–27)

In a culture of covenant, I'm not a prophet to build my own empire, my big ministry, or benefit myself. If that were true, I personally wouldn't still be pastoring a small church in north Denver that suffered a heartbreaking split in 2019. I'd be somewhere else building a following in fame and glory for my own pleasure.

I could do that and travel full-time rather than dividing my time between pastoring and itinerating. I'd be avoiding the pain and suffering of commitment to a very difficult city like Denver…but I have a covenant with the people God called me to. They matter more to me than my own life and I cannot betray that. Every word, every touch in ministry, every blessing, and every forgiveness of an offense or a wound is for the benefit of my tribe, my covenant people. What I have belongs to them. I'm not building a career for myself. I'm serving the kingdom of God.

> ANY GIFT GOD HAS GIVEN YOU IS NOT ABOUT YOU;
> IT BELONGS TO YOUR COVENANT PEOPLE FOR THEIR BENEFIT.

If you have a gift of healing, God hasn't given that to you so you have a place, position, or means of being recognized. It's not about you. The old teaching that spiritual gifts are given to make the individual important, to have place and position, is wrong. Your gift belongs to your covenant people for *their* benefit. In a culture of covenant, what you have belongs to the family. Those people are now more important than your own needs. They also stand under blood covenant obligation to regard you as more important than their needs.

If you're a teacher, it's not to advance your cause, establish your authority, or amaze everyone with your insights. It's for the building up of the people with whom you've come into covenant through Jesus.

Americans come to church to be fed, to take, and too many churches cater to that. We tend to come as consumers seeking entertainment or a product. Too many cater to that as well. We tend to come as isolated individuals with little consciousness of the impact of our own lives and actions on others. You hear very little teaching about our connectedness. The things that matter to the average American Christian revolve around what each of us feels emotionally and how we want to be made to feel.

In this modern culture, we have the same attitude toward our marriages and you don't have to be a prophet to see that it isn't working. A marriage covenant is a commitment to sacrifice my life for my mate. It's not about getting my needs met, or being blessed, or my wife making me happy. I tell every young couple for whom I perform a wedding ceremony that this is not the person you've chosen to make you happy. That's a formula for failure. You're done before you start. This is the person for whom you've chosen to lay down your life until the day that one of you dies.

My wife and I took a Myers-Briggs Type Indicator test the year we moved to Denver as part of the staff of the large church where I was executive pastor for fourteen months. When the results came back, they indicated that we were such opposites that the tester said, "You two shouldn't even be together, but obviously, you've worked out the issues." I responded, "What issues?"

I was the hippie. She was the nerd. We didn't like the same music. I was playing "Purple Haze" and she'd been singing, "In my sweet little Alice blue gown..." with her mother all her life. Our personalities are diametric opposites. I laughed until I cried watching the movie Porky's, while she muttered, "That's not funny, hubby." I jaywalk when we go to Estes Park at the foot of Rocky Mountain National Park and then wait for her on the other side of the street while she goes to the corner to wait for the light. On and on it goes.

We've been happily married for forty-eight years, not because we're so compatible, or because we've always met one another's needs, or because we never had a problem, but because of blood covenant. She is more important to me than me, I am more important to her than her, and we act on it. It's a blood covenant. As we do that, real love grows. Real joy. Real peace.

And it can never be threatened or broken. How I affect her is more important to me than how she affects me. That's what happens when you pass through the halves of the blood sacrifice in a figure eight and exchange places. The blood covenant is an exchange of life. What matters is how my actions affect you, my family—you, whom I would defend with my life because that's what the covenant means.

Jesus defended us with His life while we were yet offenders. That's what covenant people do. We've passed in a figure eight between the halves of the sacrifice of Jesus's body and blood, exchanging places with one another and with our Savior through the body of Jesus, through His blood that does more than cleanse us from sin. His blood is covenant blood and it bonds us, not just to Him, but to one another. *"This cup"* that we share in Communion *"is the new covenant in My blood"* (Luke 22:20).

> ### JESUS'S BLOOD IS COVENANT BLOOD THAT BONDS US, NOT JUST TO HIM, BUT TO ONE ANOTHER.

For lack of a foundation in covenant, the church fails and lives are destroyed.

COVENANT RULES OUT ISOLATION

Recent years have been difficult for many of the Lord's people. I have connections all over the nation and the world. People have messaged me and called me with stories of hurts, disappointments, disasters, and even broken relationships. We've not really grasped the foundational importance of a culture of covenant, so most people just isolate. They cut themselves off from others.

In isolation, their situations and unhappiness only become worse because God never designed us to work that way.

Someone once asked me, "What is the root of this tendency to isolate?" I answered that in this culture, we have no understanding of what covenant means. We're steeped in consumerism and a focus on self, the worship of our emotions.

> A CULTURE OF COVENANT EDIFIES AND STRENGTHENS, WHILE A CULTURE OF SELF WEAKENS AND DESTROYS.

A culture of covenant and the culture of self stand diametrically opposed to one another. One cancels the other. One edifies and strengthens, while the other weakens and destroys.

The heart of the book of Hebrews speaks of the better covenant we have in Jesus. It is simply an extension of the blood covenant with Abraham, and it leads to this:

Let us hold fast the confession of our hope without wavering, for He who promised is faithful; and let us consider how to stimulate one another to love and good deeds, not forsaking our own assembling together, as is the habit of some, but encouraging one another; and all the more as you see the day drawing near.   (Hebrews 10:23–25)

Read this passage carefully. You cannot maintain unwavering hope apart from commitment to a culture of covenant connection with God's people, based in the better blood covenant Jesus gave us. A culture of covenant encourages, uplifts, stands with, and practices presence for one another. It leads us to grow in doing great things. It's a sharing of life, of sacrifice for one another. In a culture of covenant, you do not, therefore, isolate. You refuse to forsake the gathering because in the gathering, you give yourself for the sake of others to encourage them, lift them, and stimulate them to a better life of sacrifice. In the blood covenant, with the economy of God, when you give yourself away, you feed your own joy and strength because now you matter to someone else. That's how covenant life works.

A CULTURE OF COVENANT DRIVES US TO LOVE EACH OTHER WITH THE FATHER'S HEART.

Without a foundation in covenant, the culture of honor has no meaning. It's just words. Without a foundation in covenant culture, the Father's heart will mean only that the Father God loves *me*, but it won't drive me to love *you* with His heart. That's where blood covenant takes us. That's how God designed the world to work. You can try to make it work some other way if you want, but you might as well try to fly by flapping your elbows.

Blood covenant forms the foundation on which the last days outpouring of the Holy Spirit must rest. Without it, pulses of God's Spirit may come, and brief outbursts of revival may happen, but they cannot last. The last days outpouring of the Holy Spirit leads us to return to the ancient ways of the blood covenant with Abraham.

Thus says the LORD, *"Stand by the ways and see and ask for the ancient paths, where the good way is, and walk in it; and you will find rest for your souls."*   (Jeremiah 6:16)

POSTSCRIPT

Earlier in this book, I spoke of a blending of Old Testament prophetic ministry with New Testament prophetic ministry. I have never ascribed to the idea that somehow the New Testament cancels the old or that there should be a real difference in ministry outlined in one testament as opposed to the other. Each illuminates the other—because God never changes.

In this writing, I have therefore tried to fulfill the calling of the Old Testament prophets to sort the precious from the vile, polluted worship from pure devotion, and good from evil. I take issue with those who limit prophecy today to the 1 Corinthians 14:3 list—edification, exhortation, and comfort. Paul meant to illustrate, not limit, the prophetic function. "Say only nice things, encouraging things," will not get us where we're going. There remains a burden on true prophetic voices *"to pluck up and to break down, to destroy and to overthrow, to build and to plant"* (Jeremiah 1:10).

On balance, however, the functions of prophetic ministry outlined in the New Testament must be taken into account. Agabus prepared the early church for the famine to come by prophesying its approach. He prepared the apostle Paul for his imprisonment in Rome by warning what would happen if he went down to Jerusalem. The 1 Corinthians list is certainly valid and necessary for lifting and motivating the body of Christ. In fact, even the Old Testament prophets delivered their dire words of destruction for Israel infused with hope, promises of restoration, and glory to come.

I have therefore tried to speak from the whole counsel of God's word, wedding the functions of the Old Testament prophetic word with the functions of New Testament prophecy. Although I may have offended some along the way, this was not my intention. I wish to dishonor no one, but rather to express differing viewpoints with both respect and honor. For this reason, I have mentioned no one by name except in the context of honor, never in disagreement.

Much of what I have written may not be popular. I've learned from the Lord never to allow that kind of consideration to determine what I speak. There is a difference between what people want to hear and what God wants them to hear. Similarly there is a difference between speaking to the people to meet their perceived needs and speaking from God for what He says they need. To this, I have tried to be faithful.

If I've missed it on some points, I apologize in advance. If I've hit the nail on the head, then please heed my words. In any case, we who love Jesus are all brothers and sisters from the same Father. Let us by all means walk in love.

ABOUT THE AUTHOR

R. Loren Sandford grew up a preacher's son in the Congregational Church in Illinois, Kansas, and north Idaho. As a teenager, he played rock music professionally in three states as well as two Canadian provinces before attending the College of Idaho. In 1973, he earned his B.A. in Music Education, then moved to California and attended Fuller Theological Seminary in Pasadena, where he earned a Master of Divinity degree in 1976.

Since 1976, Loren has served four churches full-time, successfully planting two of them himself, including New Song Church and Ministries in Denver, Colorado, where he remains the senior pastor. In 1979 and 1980, he co-directed Elijah House, an international ministry in Christian counseling and counselor training. Initially ordained in a mainline denomination, where he served on the national board for the charismatic renewal group within that affiliation, Loren served in the Vineyard from 1988 through 1992. In 1991, he was the worship leader for the first Promise Keepers mass men's meeting at the CU Event Center in Boulder, Colorado. Until 2013, he was affiliated with Partners in Harvest, an association of churches associated with the Toronto Airport Christian Fellowship (now known as Catch the Fire Toronto) and the renewal centered there. Loren served for fourteen years as a member of the International Input Council for Partners in Harvest and oversaw the central western region for that family of churches.

He travels internationally, teaching and speaking for conferences in renewal churches, and overseeing and advising ministries in various capacities. He serves as a prophetic advisor and board vice chairman for Elijah Rain Ministries.

Loren has released seventeen albums of original music, most of it for worship. Other books he has authored include *Purifying the Prophetic: Breaking Free from the Spirit of Self-Fulfillment; Understanding Prophetic People: Blessings and Problems with the Prophetic Gift; Wielding the Power to Change Your World; Renewal for the Wounded Warrior: A Burnout Survival Guide for Believers; Visions of the Coming Days: What to Look for and How to Prepare; Yes There's More: A Return to a Childlike Faith and a Deeper Experience of God;* and *A Vision of Hope for the End Times: Why I Want to Be Left Behind.* He coauthored, with Jeremiah Johnson, *The Micaiah Company: A Prophetic Reformation.*

Loren and his wife, Beth, wed in 1972. They have three grown children and eleven grandchildren. Loren is also a member of the Osage Nation, a Native American tribe centered in Oklahoma.